Perspectives on Pacifism

Also in the *Perspectives Series*

Religious Perspectives on War: Christian, Muslim, and Jewish Attitudes toward Force after the Gulf War, by David R. Smock

Islam and Democracy: Religion, Politics, and Power in the Middle East, by Timothy Sisk

Conflict Resolution in the Middle East: Simulating a Diplomatic Negotiation between Israel and Syria, by J. Lewis Rasmussen and Robert B. Oakley

PERSPECTIVES ON PACIFISM

Christian, Jewish, and Muslim Views on Nonviolence and International Conflict

DAVID R. SMOCK

Introduction by David Little

UNITED STATES INSTITUTE OF PEACE PRESS
Washington, D.C.

The views expressed in this book are those of the author and seminar participants alone. They do not necessarily reflect views of the United States Institute of Peace.

United States Institute of Peace
1550 M Street, N.W.
Washington, D.C. 20005-1708

First published 1995

Printed in the United States of America

The paper used in this publication meets the minimum requirements of American National Standard for Information Sciences—Permanence of Paper for Printed Library Materials, ANSI Z39.48-1984.

Library of Congress Cataloging-in-Publication Data
Smock, David R.
    Perspectives on pacifism: Christian, Jewish, and Muslim views on nonviolence and international conflict / David R. Smock.
        p. cm.
    Based on a symposium held July 28, 1993, sponsored by the United States Institute of Peace.
    Includes bibliographical references.
    ISBN 1-878379-42-9 : (pbk. : alk. paper)
    1. Nonviolence—Religious aspects—Comparative studies—Congresses. 2. Pacifism—Religious aspects—Comparative studies—Congresses. 3. War—Religious aspects—Comparative studies—Congresses. 4. Peace—Religious aspects—Comparative studies—Congresses. I. United States Institute of Peace. II. Title.
BL65.V55S66 1994
291.1'7873—dc20   94-45230
                                                                          CIP

Contents

Summary

Nonviolent political action has gained renewed attention in recent years as an approach to resolving international conflicts and facilitating peaceful transitions from authoritarian regimes in places such as Czechoslovakia, East Germany, Poland, and the Philippines. Moreover, some argue that "major war" is obsolescent, giving added significance to nonviolence as a mechanism for political change.

In this environment, religious groups that are the main keepers of the faith in pacifism have sought opportunities to discuss and debate nonviolent approaches to conflict resolution in the rapidly evolving international system. But as violent horrors have unfolded in such countries as Bosnia, Somalia, and Rwanda, pacifists and other advocates of nonviolence have been hard pressed to offer viable nonviolent options for peacemaking. Moreover, critics of pacifism point to the severe limitations of nonviolent action in achieving just and stable solutions in these situations and elsewhere.

As a follow-up to an earlier symposium on religious perspectives on war, the United States Institute of Peace organized a one-day symposium in July 1993 on religious perspectives on pacifism. Special consideration was given to what pacifism and nonviolent political action have to offer today to international peacemaking and conflict resolution. Participants included leading theologians and practitioners of nonviolence, as well as religious scholars and analysts inclined toward the "just war" position, which holds that violence is justified as a last resort under prescribed conditions. To encourage interfaith dialogue, papers and discussions encompassed Christian, Jewish, and Muslim perspectives.

Although such a diverse group of participants reached consensus on only a few issues, some important insights emerged that help illuminate the complex issues under discussion and provide the basis for further analysis:

- The pacifist tradition is stronger in Christianity than in the other two faiths, but there are Jewish and Muslim pacifists as well. Moreover, even the nonpacifists in the three faiths generally agree that force should be avoided whenever possible. Peace and the resolution of violent conflict are highly valued by all three faiths.

- All three faiths face similar dilemmas with regard to violence, in that they understand God to be asking humanity both to eschew violence and to promote justice, which many believe cannot always be achieved nonviolently.

- Although all three faiths have honored traditions of quietistic withdrawal and even submission under special circumstances, nonviolence should not be equated with passive acquiescence but seen as an active means of legitimate intervention to promote justice and reconciliation.

- Pacifists and those who advocate use of force as a last resort disagreed regarding the legitimacy of violent measures in international peacemaking, but all agreed that more can be done in the following areas:
  - Promoting reconciliation and conflict resolution skills
  - Using teams of nonviolent peacemakers, either alone or as adjuncts to armed peacekeepers
  - Advancing peace in areas of conflict through work with religious bodies and communities

- A pacifist participant set forth a proposal for a nonviolent Peaceforce to be created under the aegis of the United Nations as the principal mechanism for international peacemaking and peacekeeping. Some participants criticized this proposal as utopian and unrealistic.

- By the end of the discussion there was noticeable movement toward greater consensus, with some just war advocates conceding significant limitations in their perspective and some pacifists noting shortcomings in theirs. Advocates on both sides are committed to reducing violence, and they need each other to think through these issues in a creative and religiously authentic fashion and to jointly discover new means of promoting peace throughout the world.

Perspectives on Pacifism

betokens the actor's eagerness to share the cost and bear the burden of achieving peace by voluntarily accepting abuse and deprivation, without retaliating. Finally, nonviolence involves noncooperation with evil. It is action intended to defy and resist injustice without using the violent means by which injustice is typically enforced.[3]

King articulated these five characteristics of nonviolence: (1) Nonviolence does resist. "It is nonaggressive physically but dynamically aggressive spiritually." (2) Nonviolence "does not seek to defeat or humiliate the opponent," but to win the opponent's understanding through awakening a sense of moral shame so as to reconstruct the "beloved community." (3) Nonviolence is "directed against forces of evil rather than against persons who are caught in those forces." (4) Nonviolence seeks to avoid not only "external physical violence but also internal violence of spirit." (5) Nonviolence is "based on the conviction that the universe is on the side of justice."[4]

Pacifism, in turn, is a doctrine or set of doctrines indicating why and when nonviolence should be used, usually on moral or religious grounds. "Absolute," or "strict," pacifism stands for "principled nonviolence." It is advocated by those who believe that one's behavior should be nonviolent as a matter of principle, not simply as a result of a calculation of the effectiveness of nonviolence as a technique or instrument. Many people who do not subscribe to absolute pacifism nevertheless advocate nonviolent behavior under certain circumstances. They are sometimes called "pragmatic," or "situational," pacifists. For example, nuclear pacifists believe that nonviolence is preferable to the threat or use of nuclear weapons, since the uncontrollable destructiveness of nuclear weapons renders them unusable from a moral point of view. On the other hand, nuclear pacifists are not necessarily opposed to conventional military action. By contrast, principled nonviolence rests on the conviction that violence should always be avoided because it is wrong and morally repugnant in itself.

A significant, even growing, group advocates nonviolence not on the basis of principle or religious faith, but as the most effective instrument to wage a struggle for social transformation and change. Some advocates of this form of instrumental nonviolence term it the "technique approach" to nonviolence.[5] As a leader in the struggle against apartheid in South Africa, Anglican archbishop Desmond Tutu advocated nonviolence as an indispensable strategic tool and one consistent with Christian principles, but his belief in the limitations of nonviolence led him to hold open the option of violence as another means to confront and overcome the evils of apartheid. Advocates of the technique approach may support nonviolent behavior in all instances, but they differ from advocates of principled nonviolence in that their motivation is based on the likely effectiveness of nonviolence rather than a religious or moral principle that forbids the use of violence.

A further distinction must be made between types of nonviolence and pacifism. Some of the contributors to the discussion reported in this book, like Walter Wink, underscore their belief that pacifism and nonviolence should not be passive. Rather, nonviolence should constitute a kind of resistance, the intent of which is social and political transformation. Wink has written elsewhere: "Christians have all too often called for 'nonviolence' when they really meant tranquility. Nonviolence, in fact, seeks out conflict, elicits conflict, exacerbates conflict, in order to bring it out into the open and lance its poisonous sores. It is not idealistic or sentimental about evil; it does not coddle or cajole aggressors, but moves against perceived injustice proactively, with the same alacrity as the most hawkish militarist."[6] King's advocacy of civil disobedience and noncooperation with evil exemplify this proactive approach.

On the other hand, other participants in the discussion point out that in all three faiths considered (Christianity, Judaism, and Islam) one can identify traditions of passive nonviolence or quietism. As Yehudah Mirsky points out, in Judaism this strand of passive nonviolence is sometimes expressed in martyrdom. Passive nonviolence may also be lived out in withdrawal from society into religious enclaves, such as monasteries. Those who adopt passive nonviolence are usually led to that position by an assessment that neither violence nor nonviolent resistance is likely to effectively combat the evil they confront.

Many other types of pacifism could also be described. John Howard Yoder has identified twenty-nine.[7]

If nonviolence attracts new interest, it also faces difficult challenges. Is nonviolence, after all, the answer to the shocking examples of brutality and oppression in places like Bosnia, Somalia, Sudan, and Haiti? Is it possible to restrain such inhumanity without using force? Can international justice be achieved if force is prohibited? Many proponents admit deep ambivalence. They have grave doubts about the efficacy of force in such situations, but neither are they sure about the feasibility or the effectiveness of purely nonviolent responses to such catastrophes. Of course, many advocates of force share the same kind of bewilderment about how force might be used to promote peace in situations like Rwanda and Bosnia. Moreover, the use of force by the United States and the United Nations in Somalia was far from uniformly successful.

Because of the new interest as well as the perplexity that surrounds the use of nonviolence in international affairs, it seems a fitting time to explore the question afresh. Moreover, because religious people have frequently been proponents and leaders of nonviolent movements and have given extensive attention to the grounds and tactics of nonviolence, it is appropriate to accord them a prominent role in discussing the subject.

In fact, there is within the religious community a new appreciation of nonviolence and a new devotion to thinking through how nonviolent tactics ought to be implemented. As the National Conference of Catholic Bishops remarked in a recent public statement,

> Although nonviolence has often been regarded as simply a personal option or vocation, recent history suggests that in some circumstances it can be an effective public undertaking as well. Dramatic political transitions in places as diverse as the Philippines and Eastern Europe demonstrate the power of nonviolent action, even against dictatorial and totalitarian regimes. . . . One must ask, in the light of recent history, whether nonviolence should be restricted to personal commitments or whether it also should have a place in the public order with the tradition of justified and limited war. National leaders bear a moral obligation to see that alternative techniques for dealing with conflicts are seriously considered. . . . As a nation we have an affirmative obligation to promote research and education in nonviolent means of resisting evil. We need to address nonviolent strategies with much greater seriousness in international affairs.[8]

The United States Institute of Peace convened a day-long conference on July 28, 1993, gathering thirty-one specialists on religious attitudes toward nonviolence. Affirming the value of interfaith dialogue, the Institute invited representatives of very diverse points of view from all three Abrahamic faiths. This gathering followed an earlier conference, held in March 1992, that addressed a related subject: Christian, Jewish, and Islamic perspectives on the use of force in the aftermath of the Gulf War of 1991.[9]

As the Institute's senior scholar in religion, ethics, and human rights, I chaired the session. The discussion was structured around five papers and four responses.[10] The first paper presented a Christian case for strongly preferring nonviolence; it was followed by a response from a Christian advocate of the just war tradition. The second paper argued that while Judaism honors nonviolent action under some conditions, it permits and even enjoins the use of force in defense of the survival of the Jewish community. In response, a Jewish pacifist stressed the centrality of nonviolence in Judaism.

The third paper contended that although Islam permits the use of force, force must be constrained by a prior disposition toward peace, and under some circumstances, nonviolence, understood as "quietism," is explicitly recommended. A pacifist who is knowledgeable about Islam responded by describing an example of nonviolent commitment by one prominent Muslim. The fourth paper drew some comparative conclusions concerning nonviolence among the three faiths. The last paper, by a Christian pacifist, proposed a nonviolent strategy for intervention in international conflicts.

The discussion focused on two basic issues. The first was whether and to what degree nonviolence is a resource for peacemaking in each of the three faiths. How do the Christian, Muslim, and Jewish traditions understand nonviolence and work with it? Are there warrants in the three traditions for taking an absolute stand on the subject, or do the traditions favor a more selective approach? If selective, what are the conditions for using and not using violence?

While there are decided differences both among and within the traditions, all three, as the discussion made clear, reveal deep respect for nonviolent action and considerable reluctance to turn to force. There would seem to be the makings here of a common, or at least similar, spirit, and perhaps that spirit can provide the basis for cooperative thinking and acting in the future. While certain strands of Christianity—some of them eloquently represented at the conference— take an absolute position in favor of nonviolence, other Christians do not. There does not appear to be the same degree of support within Judaism or Islam for an absolute or near-absolute commitment to nonviolence, but the position has some advocates. As for those participants defending only the selective use of nonviolence, Christians, Jews, and Muslims all tended to revert to a shared allegiance to something close to traditional just war standards.

The second issue concerned the applicability of the teaching about nonviolence to various contemporary international conflicts. How might the attitudes toward nonviolence presented in the three traditions be employed in Bosnia, Somalia, and similar situations? Is force ever permitted? If so, how is force to be used in connection with nonviolence? If not, what are the specific nonviolent tactics that follow from the traditions?

Here the discussion took shape in response to the final paper—the stimulating proposal by a Christian pacifist (John Paul Lederach) for creating an international "Peaceforce" as a means for nonviolent resolution of the conflicts in Bosnia, Somalia, Haiti, and so forth. The proposal generated lively and at times intense debate over its desirability and feasibility. The cleavages in the debate cut across the three traditions, often dividing more in accord with a predisposition toward nonviolence than with religious identity.

Though the central questions were not resolved, the participants, by common acknowlegment, developed deeper appreciation for the range of positions advocated, and they expressed enthusiasm for interfaith consideration of such sensitive and important topics.

The following synopsis of the discussion, written with his customary proficiency and lucidity by David R. Smock, roughly matches the sequence of the presentations and debate. The first four chapters consider the role of nonviolence and pacifism in the three faiths. The remaining chapters focus on the appropriateness and potential effectiveness of nonviolent approaches to resolving international conflict.

2

Nonviolence and Pacifism within Christian Thought

Contemporary Christian pacifism finds its principal roots in the Anabaptist community that emerged as a movement in Zurich in 1524. The Anabaptists advocated the formation of voluntary and disciplined faith communities and the rejection of both violence and participation in government.[11] They extolled the way of life of the early church and contended that the way of Jesus Christ contradicts the sinfulness of the world to the point that true Christians should avoid participation in worldly institutions. The Christian community ought to be perfectionist, separatist, and pacifist, and the standard of behavior is to follow Christ. Some groups of Anabaptists, like the Hutterian Brethren, also shared their possessions.

Menno Simons (1496–1561) did much through his writings and leadership to establish the Anabaptist believing community. In such works as *Foundations of Christian Doctrine*[12] he rejected the use of violence by Christians as an expression of their obedience to the suffering Christ but recognized that the sword has a use outside the Christian fellowship. Lisa Sowle Cahill writes, "Although it is certain that he means the followers of Jesus to rely only upon the 'sword of the Spirit' in self-defense and the reproof of wickedness, Menno nonetheless appeals to the civil authorities for relief, arguing as Tertullian and Origen had before him that the separatist Christians are not seditious."[13] The deep and lasting influence of Menno Simons and the Anabaptist movement can be seen in the life and faith of contempory

Mennonites, Amish, and Hutterrian Brethren, particularly in their
shared way of life and their commitment to biblical nonviolence.

The Religious Society of Friends (the Quakers) emerged in seven-
teenth-century England and eighteenth-century North America and
articulated a strict form of pacifism based on adherence to Christ's
teachings and the nature of the Kingdom of God that Christ articulated. Enemies are to be loved, not attacked. Acts of nonviolence can
advance the Kingdom and promote the conversion of others. While
not as thorough as the Anabaptists in their rejection of secular society,
the Quakers "did not see participation in structures of violence as
appropriate for those in whom Christ dwells. Instead, they expected
total regeneration of life through God's grace, and took as seriously as
the Anabaptists the Christian mission to convert the world and to
transform it."[14] George Fox, who shaped much of the early theology
of the Quakers, identified himself as "the son of God sent to stand a
witness against all violence" asserting that his "weapons are not carnal
but spiritual."[15]

In summarizing her analysis of the historical roots of contemporary
Christian pacifism, Cahill writes that such groups as the Anabaptists
and Quakers "all in some way bypass institutional forms of religion and
try to re-create New Testament religious fervor and immediacy of
Jesus. Physical force and especially war drive against Christ's cross,
salvation, mercy, and charity, and are acutely impossible in service of a
religious cause."[16] Jesus' teachings and moral demands put within
reach a new life of unity with Christ reflecting the Kingdom of God. A
life of faithful and peaceful discipleship will necessarily result in cross-
bearing sacrifice and suffering for those who practice nonviolence.

In the twentieth century the principal theorists of Christian pacifism include Walter Rauschenbusch, the primary theologian of the
social gospel. Reflecting his pacifism, Rauschenbusch viewed World
War I as a violation of everything Christianity stands for. In 1917 he
called for a "Christianizing of international relations."[17] For
Rauschenbusch, war caused enormous and irreparable harm to the
people involved and violated Jesus' injunctions to create a harmonious
kingdom among all peoples.

Cahill cites a 1932 issue of the *Christian Century* as carrying an illuminating and influential debate on pacifism between the Niebuhr

brothers, with H. Richard Niebuhr articulating a pacifist position and Reinhold Niebuhr defending just war in relation to intervention in Manchuria. The debate joins two critical questions for contemporary Christians. "First, is coercion really necessary to accomplish historically the responsibility to neighbor that the gospel enjoins? Second, and perhaps more important, what is the truly Christian motive for pacifism: active love that seeks to improve the human lot, or obedient fidelity that seeks simply to do as Christ did and as he demands?"[18]

More recently, Dorothy Day of the Catholic Worker Movement and the Trappist monk Thomas Merton have been influential advocates of pacifism from a Catholic perspective, as have James and Shelley Douglass of Ground Zero Center for Nonviolent Action and Gordon Zahn. John Howard Yoder and Stanley Hauerwas have been among the most important Protestant pacifist theologians.

The debate is clearly of long standing, but the issues remain, and they were articulately presented and argued at the July 1993 conference. Do the Christian Scriptures oblige Christians to adopt a position of principled and absolute pacifism? Is the Christian just war tradition consistent with the basic tenets of the Christian faith? Might there be a third way, which adopts the best of both the just war and the pacifist positions?

Professor Walter Wink of Auburn Theological Seminary, formerly a Peace Fellow of the United States Institute of Peace, opened the discussion with a paper entitled "Beyond Just War and Pacifism," advocating nonviolence as the only authentic Christian option. Wink noted that Gandhi contended that the only people on earth who do not see Christ and his teachings as nonviolent are Christians.

Over the past four centuries, a period during which 140 million persons have been killed in war, the peace churches have kept alive the gospel's witness against war. Most of these deaths have occurred in the twentieth century, and two-thirds occurred in "Christian" Europe. In recent years, Wink argued, nonviolence has been employed with greater frequency and effectiveness. He pointed out that in 1989 alone, thirteen nations experienced nonviolent revolutions, and all except the one in China were successful. In contrast to the usual complaint that nonviolence doesn't work, Wink contended that it has been working remarkably well.

Wink's advocacy of nonviolence is rooted in the teachings of Jesus. Unfortunately, according to Wink, both pacifists and just war advocates have based their positions on a misunderstanding of key verses of Scripture. Many pacifists have misinterpreted Jesus' teaching found in Matt. 5:39 ("Do not resist one who is evil") as implying that nonresistance is the appropriate Christian response to evil and that nonresistance means passivity, withdrawal, and submissiveness. The correct translation is "Do not repay evil for evil," consistent with Rom. 12:17, 1 Thess. 5:15, and 1 Pet. 3:9. "Jesus is not, therefore, telling us to capitulate to evil, but to refuse to oppose it on its own terms. He is urging us to avoid mirroring evil, to refuse to let the opponent dictate the methods of our opposition." Far from counseling submissiveness in the face of evil, Jesus is urging that we stand up to evil but resist nonviolently. Jesus' nonviolence is coercive, but it is not lethal or injurious. Jesus' admonition to turn the other cheek when someone strikes you does not mean that Christians are to allow an assailant to pummel them. Jesus is urging victims of oppression to "stand up for yourselves, take control of your responses, don't answer the oppressor in kind, but find a new, third way that is neither cowardly submission nor violent reprisal."

Wink interprets Matt. 5:40 as counseling the poor not to be awed by the power and wealth of the rulers. "By refusing to be awed by their power, the powerless are emboldened to seize the initiative, even where structural change is not immediately possible. This message, far from being a counsel to unattainable perfection, is a practical, strategic measure for empowering the oppressed, and it is being lived out all over the world today by powerless people ready to take their history into their own hands" by engaging in nonviolent resistance.

Jesus does not advocate armed revolution, but rather a social revolution, according to Wink. Jesus admonished that we "not react violently to evil; do not counter evil in kind; do not let evil dictate the terms of your opposition; do not let violence draw you into imitative rivalry." This is the revolutionary principle that Jesus articulated as the basis for nonviolent resistance, a form of resistance that is proactive, aggressive, and courageous. It is a form of confronting evil with great potential for personal and social transformation. "Jesus abhors both passivity and violence. He articulates out of the history of his own people's struggles, a way by which evil can be opposed without being mirrored, the oppressor resisted without being emulated, and the enemy neutralized without being destroyed."

The new reality that Jesus proclaimed was evident in his entire life and teaching and the way he faced death. Wink noted that it was not a tactical or pragmatic nonviolence; Jesus saw nonviolence "as a direct corollary of the nature of God and of the new reality emerging in the world from God." Nonviolence is a quality of the Kingdom of God, not just a means to attain the Kingdom. "Those who live nonviolently are already manifesting the transformed reality of the divine order now."

Wink then turned to consider pacifism in relation to just war theory. While he has not witnessed a groundswell of new converts to pacifism, he has been aware of growing dissatisfaction with just war theory and of a deeply felt desire to move beyond it. After the Cold War and the madness of the arms race, many people "have become skeptical of the just war tradition's capacity to be honest in the face of pressures to support national positions based more on national self-interest than on ethical principles." Wink's problem is not with the just war criteria themselves, but with "the fact that they have been subordinated to the myth of redemptive violence: the belief that violence saves." Just war theorists often object to the perfectionism of pacifists, since the pacifist insistence on ethical means sometimes seems to obscure the demand for justice. Pacifists, on the other hand, often criticize just war theorists as serving as propagandists for war machines, "providing moral legitimacy for military interventions motivated by the needs of empire." While just war theorists are often thought to be accommodating, pacifists are frequently charged with being irresponsible.

References to "just war" ought to be eliminated, Wink contended. The word "pacifism" inappropriately conveys passivity, and "just war" incorrectly implies that war is justifiable. Although faithful Christians cannot talk of "just war," they also cannot completely disregard just war criteria. They cannot "wish away a world of bewildering complexity, in which difficult decisions are forced on us by the violence of others, and where nonviolent solutions are not always forthcoming." For Wink the theory need not be jettisoned, since it has real value in its capacity to help us think morally about the conditions in which war is conducted. However, it ought to be applied within a commitment to nonviolence.

There may be, Wink asserted, a third way—one that affirms the pacifist's nonviolence and the just war theorist's concern for moral accountability in times of war. Such a position requires a prior commitment to nonviolence combined with a more rigorous use of the just war criteria than is usual. Consistent with this position, Wink suggested adopting the phrase "violence reduction criteria" to replace "just war criteria." The new approach would be aimed at avoiding warfare or decreasing its horrors once it begins, within an overall commitment to nonviolence. Those adopting this position would call on governments to wage war with less barbarism and ferocity. This position would permit moral consideration and reflection on war without providing moral justification for warfare.

Wink recognized significant common ground between nonviolence/pacifism and just war theory. "Both acknowledge that nonviolence is preferable to violence. Both agree that the innocent must be protected as much as possible. Both reject any defense of a war motivated solely by a crusade mentality or national security interests or personal egocentricity. Both wish to persuade states to reduce the levels of violence. Both wish to hold war accountable to moral values, both before and during the conflict."

Violence reduction criteria might provide "prudential moral leverage on political leaders for whom the language of the gospel carries no conviction." Wink contended that what he advocates is a return to the ancient position of the church. The early Christians, according to Wink, opposed all wars, but they nevertheless made distinctions between wars, based on the conviction that humane treatment of the enemy was superior to cruelty.

Wink concluded by arguing that it is possible to move beyond the old arguments between pacifism and just war. Christians must recognize that Jesus is against all forms of violence and domination and that nonviolence is a fundamental tenet of the gospel of God's in-breaking new order. From this position of principled nonviolence, just war criteria can be transformed into violence reduction criteria for limiting the devastation of a war.

In response, Richard Land of the Southern Baptist Convention commended Wink's presentation for its emphasis on the sometimes provocative and often assertive and nonpassive nature of pacifism and nonviolence. Nonviolence engages the adversary and seeks to change. The most notable example was the civil rights movement led by Martin Luther King, Jr., in which King provocatively engaged and challenged the hypocrisy of many people of faith in the South and forced them to confront their own prejudices.

There are many situations of international injustice, Land pointed out, that could usefully be addressed through nonviolent means. But when these opportunities are missed and the situation becomes desperate, the chance for effective nonviolence may be lost. We must "understand our responsibilities in relation to Psalm 82:4, to rescue the weak and needy and deliver them from the hand of the wicked, and there comes a point at which the only way to deliver them from the hands of the Gestapo and the SS is to use force."

As an advocate of the just war tradition, Land recalled that its principal standards—just cause, just intent, last resort, legitimate authority, limited goals, proportionality, and noncombatant immunity—are used to determine whether a given use of force is justifiable. According to the tradition, violence may not be excluded in the struggle against evil; at the same time, it may be used only under the strictest constraints.

Land agreed with Wink that the just war tradition has often been misused. Almost all wars in recent memory fail to meet just war standards, either in theory or in practice, but the tradition is frequently invoked to rationalize war and is used to distract people from seeking "proactive peacemaking solutions." Those who uncritically embrace just war thinking run the risk of becoming addicted to force. For Land, Israel was fully justified in defending itself in 1948, but since that time the Israelis have relied overmuch on military power as a way of resolving their differences with the Palestinians.

Accordingly, regard for the benefits of nonviolent action is an important corrective to the potential excesses of just war thinking. In that way, considerable common ground exists between principled nonviolence and a conscientious use of just war theory. On the other hand, there are points at which the two approaches diverge, and a choice must be made between them. In Land's view, such a point has been reached in the case of Bosnia, where "ethnic cleansing" by Serb forces against Croats and Muslims should not be tolerated by the international community. In that setting, nothing short of multinational armed intervention has a chance of producing a just peace.

Challenging Wink's contention that the early Christians were opposed to all wars, John Kelsay of Florida State University asserted that material available on the early Christians is very limited and inconclusive. From what is known, however, it is more accurate to say that the early Christians refused to participate in wars, rather than saying that they opposed all wars, and that is a significant difference. Kelsay was also puzzled by Wink's radical reinterpretation of certain biblical passages and wondered how the tradition has misunderstood Jesus in such a thoroughgoing manner for two millennia.

In response to Wink's suggested transformation of just war criteria into violence reduction criteria, Kelsay concluded that this might be a creative idea but that such a transformation might misconstrue the intended purpose of just war criteria. He pointed out that just war thinking is really more concerned with helping societies discern when resort to war is justified than with limiting or reducing violence. Beyond that, just war criteria are guidelines for the wise use of power.

Supporting Kelsay's point, John Langan of Georgetown University said that if the standards are to be renamed, then it will be necessary to speak not only of "violence reduction criteria," but of "violence authorization criteria" as well. Langan also cautioned against the "perfectionist" interpretation of the just war criteria preferred by Wink. A perfectionist interpretation undermines the criteria, because any infringement of the criteria, however minor, "means that the whole game is off and one cannot legitimately participate." According to Langan, Wink's readiness to condemn violence and at the same time to condone its use, so long as it is sufficiently "reduced," reflects a significant divergence between Catholic and Protestant ways of thinking. Wink's position seems more consistent with a Protestant emphasis on moral ambiguity, in contrast to Catholic impatience with such an emphasis.

Russell Hittinger of the American Enterprise Institute criticized Wink's embrace of principled nonviolence by asserting that peace and violence are not in themselves moral properties. Peace and violence cannot be adequately considered or debated without introducing the concept of justice, which is in and of itself a moral quality. Determinations of whether to employ violence must be weighed in light of justice considerations.

The most pernicious actions of this century, Hittinger asserted, have been taken to serve what has been termed "pacification," as we know from the Phoenix program in Vietnam. Lowering the threshold for violence may in the end not serve the cause of justice and may generate more devastating violence. "I think that the deceit and the inevitable violence and lack of justice that comes from these things is in a way worse than when people duke it out with bazookas," in part because full-scale violence usually ends conflicts swiftly, while pacification may go on for generations. Moreover, pacification is less amenable to moral language than warfare. War is overt, and one can consider the justice of beginning war, conducting it, and ending it. Pacification programs cannot be subjected to the same kind of moral discrimination—a point the peace community often fails to recognize.

After commending Wink for making a clear distinction between pacifism and passivity, Jay Lintner of the United Church of Christ's Office for Church in Society said that Wink's biblical interpretations give too much weight to Jesus' advocacy of defiance and challenges to the ruler. While the biblical passages about turning the other cheek and going the extra mile do contain elements of defiance, the most important feature of these teachings is Jesus' urging his flock to change the terms of the debate and to behave in ways that are counterintuitive.

Discussions of war and peace, or pacifism and violence, cannot be conducted apart from a consideration of types of governments, asserted William Morrisey of the journal *Interpretation*. States with governments that are characterized by what Morrisey terms "commercial republicanism"—that is, a free-enterprise economy with a representative form of government—almost never fight each other. "Monarchies fight amongst themselves, aristocracies fight amongst themselves, oligarchies fight amongst themselves, tyrannies fight amongst themselves, commercial republics generally do not." Most innocent civilian casualties during this century have occurred in wars perpetrated by tyrannies.

The moral analyst is obliged to ask, according to Morrisey, whether nonviolence can be effective in confronting tyrannical governments. The assertion that nonviolence was instrumental in toppling tyrannies in recent years is questionable on two counts. First, some communist regimes have been brutal in their repression of nonviolent resisters— for example, the Beijing regime at Tiananmen Square. Second, communist regimes that have been vulnerable to nonviolent opposition have been those that were in decline and had "no stomach to deal with their critics in the way they used to deal with them."

3

Jewish Perspectives

While conceding that there are some Jewish pacifists, the second paper at the conference argued that although Judaism honors nonviolent action under some conditions, it permits and even enjoins the use of force in defense of the survival of the Jewish community.

As part of his paper, Yehudah Mirsky of the Washington Institute for Near East Policy[19] posed the following questions. What does Jewish tradition direct Jews to do in matters of war and peace? Is there a way of thinking "Jewishly" about these questions, and is there a Jewish style of moral or prudential reasoning that could be of use to non-Jews?

Mirsky posited that authentic Jewish politics must meet two criteria: It "must preserve and protect the concrete interests of Jews as individuals and a community, and it must both reflect and enact the values of Jewish tradition, as embodied in both texts and history, even as it grapples with the radical newness of modern politics." As to pacifism, Mirsky concludes that Judaism rejects it. "Judaism's conception of humanity's place in the world is wholly activist, committed to the establishment of a just and Godly social order here on earth, and through worldly means. The institutions of the world, including war and statecraft, are good or evil depending on the uses to which they are put."

Mirsky further asserted that the Old Testament sees the use of force as legitimate in certain circumstances. The Sixth Commandment constitutes an injunction against murder rather than all types of killing. The spirit of the matter is best captured by the statement in Eccles. 3:8 that there is a time for war, just as there is a time for peace.

Pacifism is also rejected by Judaism, according to Mirsky, "because Judaism by its logic, nature and structure, is committed to the survival of a discrete worldly community. . . . [Thus] to the extent that the existence of the Jewish people is a religious desideratum, the steps necessary to secure that survival receive . . . religious sanction."

This is not to say that Judaism is not passionately attached to peace. Indeed, *Shalom* (peace) is regarded as one of the names of God. "The pursuit of peace is regarded as the foundation of the social order and the highest calling of the individual, and war is seen as an expression of man's sinful nature. Yet these are aspirational, and not normative, prescriptive views." Although the thrust of the Judaic law of war is to accept war as part of the life of nations, war is constrained by moral, demographic, constitutional, and ecological restrictions. Jewish legal sources also affirm the right to self-defense for both individuals and communities, if specific criteria are met.

Current Jewish thought, Mirsky noted, distinguishes between the demands of public law and private piety. Thus public policy may condone certain types of warfare, while the pietistic ideal favors nonviolence. This view is expressly articulated by Abraham Isaac Kook, jurist and theologian and the architect of religious Zionism, who says that Judaism maintains a creative, dialectical tension in order to preserve the power of the pietistic ideal, which is ultimately a matter of personal rectitude, not public policy.[20]

Still, nonviolence enjoys a place of honor in Jewish thought as an expression of personal piety and as a communal act, although the latter is expressed more in the idiom of martyrdom than as resistance per se. The underlying conception of nonviolence, one that is shared with King's doctrines of passive resistance, is that it is an important form of resistance, not a form of passivity. In Jewish thought, nonviolence "does not shrink from recognizing the reality of evil or injustice nor the imperative to combat it. Where it differs from other forms of struggle with evil, and particularly armed struggle, is in its assertion of a bond between the two sides, and in its focusing attack on the structures of evil rather than on the individuals maintaining those structures. It is not and ought not to be invoked as a justification or recipe for inaction in the face of pressing evil or injustice." Mirsky continued:

> Where the oppressor or evildoer seeks to vanquish or eradicate a victim pure and simple there is no call for nonviolence. Indeed, in that situation, nonviolence would do nothing but further empower the oppressor and force the oppressed to acquiesce in his or her own destruction,

forfeiting human dignity in the process by ceding to the oppressor the validity of his aims. The "nonviolent moment" arises only in those situations where, to begin with, the oppressor does not seek annihilation but subjugation, not destruction but the act of submission.

The relationship between the oppressor and the oppressed in the "nonviolent moment" is thus profoundly dialectical, in which each defines self in terms of the other. The oppressor's self-definition resides in the oppressed's acquiescence in political subordination, socioeconomic injustice and ideological hegemony. The self-definition of the nonviolent oppressed resides by contrast in the oppressor's perhaps flawed but still shared humanity, a humanity which makes the oppressor a full-fledged human being to whom the nonviolent testimony of the oppressed is meaningful, even if it is not fully, or just barely, understood.

Active nonviolent resistance is applicable only when organized, systemic violence is a contradiction to the logic and structure of the society. Hence, nonviolent resistance is generally inappropriate in totalitarian states where violence and oppression are embedded in the warp and woof of the society and political system.

The deepest appreciation of nonviolence in Judaism, Mirsky suggested, comes not from pietistic sources or dicta, but from the legal and nonlegal literature of martyrdom, a central and tragic aspect of Jewish existence. "The experience of persecution and martyrdom inescapably colors Judaic thinking on nonviolence and indeed on all aspects of political life." Looking to the literary sources of Jewish political thought, martyrdom—generally referred to as *Kiddush Hashem*, or sanctification of the Name—is the theme linking self-sacrifice, struggle, response to violence, and the maintenance of communal ideals.

The idea of martyrdom does not have quite the same significance in Judaism as it has in, say, Christianity. Martyrdom is of instrumental value, not called for unless essentials of group solidarity or the very fundamentals of religious belief and practice are at stake. In that case, martyrdom is positively commanded. But at other times, that kind of behavior may not be called for at all. Such a time, many Jews agree, was the period of the Holocaust, an event of indescribable evil unparalleled in human history, an ultimate threat to the very existence of the Jewish community. Martin Buber, well known for emphasizing the primacy of personal "I-Thou" relations above ethical rules, rejected Gandhi's suggestion that passive resistance by Jews could deter Hitler:

In the five years which I myself spent under the present [Nazi] regime, I observed many instances of genuine [Gandhi-like] Satyagraha among the Jews. . . . Such actions, however, exerted apparently not the slightest influence on their opponents. . . . An effective stand may be taken in the form of nonviolence against unfeeling human beings in the hope of gradually bringing them thereby to their senses; but a diabolic universal steamroller cannot thus be withstood. . . . Testimony without acknowledgement, ineffective, unobserved martyrdom, a martyrdom cast to the winds—that is the fate of innumerable Jews in Germany. . . . I do not want force. But if there is no other way of preventing the evil destroying the good, I trust I shall use force and give myself up into God's hands.[21]

At the same time, Orthodox authorities also ruled that in a genocidal situation, the demands of martyrdom often take second place to the imperatives of survival. In Mirsky's view, many Jewish scholars have arrived at a consensus over the relationship between resistance and survival in an age that threatens total annihilation of the Jews—an age, begun by the Holocaust, that may never disappear.

Mirsky concluded his paper with the following points: (1) Jewish tradition directs the Jewish community to fight against evil with whatever means are available. The community should do its utmost to preserve human life, even at the cost of subjugation and humiliation, but not at the cost of threatening the very existence of the religious and social order. (2) The Jewish style of reasoning on these issues is "highly contextual and fact-specific, informed by a rich understanding of textual warrant and historical experience, repeatedly evaluating circumstances in light of both abiding imperatives and changing circumstances." (3) The same fundamental norms apply in both Israel and the Diaspora. "The state is not absolutized or reified. . . . The sustained Jewish protest against the corruption of this world must be part of the state's ethos, even as it partakes of this world's imperfections."

A very different Jewish perspective was offered by Naomi Goodman, formerly president and currently secretary of the Jewish Peace Fellowship. For her, the mainline Jewish tradition permits violence only as a last resort, after all nonviolent alternatives have been exhausted. Even then violence is justified only in self-defense. But the focus must always remain on viable alternatives to violence and whether they have been seriously tried.

To Goodman, peace must be fundamental to Judaism, and the mainline Jewish embrace of peace does not go far enough. "Peace has always been the ideal, the messianic, the hoped for and prayed for; the goal to which we are taught to aspire, to teach our children and to lend every effort 'to seek peace and pursue it' (Ps. 34:15)." The belief in Shalom derives from the purest and highest in Jewish morality, with Shalom encompassing wholeness, righteousness, justice, grace and truth, and opposition to all killing. Shalom itself is a name of God. Although she conceded that absolute principled nonviolence was rarely demanded by the founders and interpreters of Judaism, there is a pacifist tradition within Judaism that recognizes peace as the highest priority in Jewish life and as the essence of Jewish morality.

While self-defense was permitted in biblical and rabbinical Judaism, Goodman pointed out, this permission was heavily qualified. Each life is sacred, and when a person preserves the life of one person, it is as though that person has preserved the whole world. Conversely, the person who destroys one human being is regarded as having destroyed the whole world (Mishnah Sanhedrin IV, 5). Jewish heroes are not the warriors, but the prophets and sages like Isaiah, Micah, and Habakkuk. When God is quoted in the Bible as saying "Vengeance is mine," this means that vengeance is not an appropriate response for human beings.

Goodman took issue with Mirsky's statement that Judaism rejects pacifism "not only in practice but in principle," and she contended that nonviolent direct action is a preferred means of achieving a just and godly social order. Moreover, this position has been endorsed by many noted Jewish authorities. While Mirsky claimed that the biblical commandment not to kill really means not to commit murder, Goodman argued that some Jewish authorities convincingly contend that there is no such thing as legal killing within Jewish thought. Judaism is a life-affirming religion, and the Jewish doctrine of *Imitatio Dei* signifies that humans are to be preservers of life. Goodman asserted that in Judaism neither martyrdom nor violent resistance is valued. Moreover, means and ends cannot be separated, so an evil means cannot achieve a just end.

Goodman disagrees with the distinction made in just war theory between the unacceptability of killing innocent civilians in war and the acceptability of killing those in uniform who may have taken up arms involuntarily. Why is it acceptable to kill soldiers while civilian lives are considered sacred? Is not all life sacred? She quoted Jewish authorities in defense of her position.

In closing, Goodman commended the work of Israeli Jews committed to a nonviolent defense of Israel:

> From the army officers in the Council for Peace and Security who advocate a Palestinian state as safer than the present unrest; to the soldiers in Yesh G'vul (There is a Limit) who will not serve beyond the green line which marks the Occupied Territories; to the religious Zionists in Oz veShalom/Netivot Shalom; to those who work in Arab-Jewish cooperative ventures exemplified by such projects as Interns for Peace, Neve Shalom and Givat Haviva; to the broad coalition of Peace Now and the numerous women's groups; these are Israelis who believe that "the person who turns an enemy into a friend" (Abot d'Rabbi Nathan 23) has accomplished the work of God—and protected the Jewish community.

The differences between Mirsky and Goodman may be too sharply drawn, according to Rabbi David Saperstein, director of the Religious Action Center of Reform Judaism. Mirsky's principal point is that the Jewish tradition is predominantly disposed to just war thinking, which is clearly true. For Mirsky, just war is the accepted position of mainline Judaism, but there is nevertheless a powerful tradition of nonviolence within Judaism as well. Saperstein asked whether the changing circumstances in the world require reassessment of the balance between the two traditions. It would be illuminating to consider the unique contributions Judaism might make to theologies and strategies of nonviolence and pacifism. For instance, the passionate concern within Judaism for arbitration, as opposed to only adjudication, suggests the importance of trying to resolve underlying disputes and promote mutual understanding rather than assessing solely which position is worthy and which unworthy.

Commenting on both presentations, Professor David Novak of the University of Virginia suggested that greater theological grounding is needed for some of the arguments made. He noted that Mirsky asserted that the survival of the Jewish people is an end in itself—an end worth achieving by violence, if necessary. A critical point missing from this argument, however, is the Jewish belief that Jews are the elect of

God. Being chosen by God means that Jewish survival is more critical than mere self-preservation. It has universal, even cosmic, significance. Jews are to survive to be witnesses to God's kingship and the final coming of God's kingdom on earth.

Novak objected to Goodman's citing many teachings of the Torah to bolster her assertions and interpretations without fully explicating their context. The teachings are divine injunctions offered through God's intervention in history to communicate with human beings in general and with Jewish people in particular. But without knowing the setting of each divine revelation, interpretation becomes problematic. There are canons of interpretation that determine the proper context for the interpretation of traditional texts. Without them, interpretation is arbitrarily selective.

In response, Mirsky highlighted Novak's distinction between revelation and the insightful hermeneutic that shapes normative Jewish discussion, noting that Goodman's biblical and other citations are more revelatory than insightful. At a theological level, values and divine commands judge and guide God's people, but they must be interpreted in a living Torah. Goodman's argument seems directed more toward the ideal, but an ideal that is probably not attainable, certainly not until the Jewish right to physical and corporate existence is well established.

4

An Islamic Perspective

The third paper contended that although Islam permits the use of force, force must be constrained by a prior disposition toward peace, and under some circumstances, nonviolence, understood as "quietism," is explicitly recommended. Moreover, some Sufi mystics are pacifists.

Professor Abdulaziz Sachedina of the University of Virginia explained that the Islamic attitude toward pacifism and nonviolence must be viewed in context, particularly in terms of the social and historical circumstances of seventh-century Arabia. Pre-Islamic Arabia was a tribal society that valued the status quo; life represented an eternal cycle of repetition. The principal ambition was to bring glory and honor to the tribe according to custom. Whatever brought shame to the tribe was evil. Many people were oppressed. Women were property, and there was serious imbalance between the rich and the poor.

In this setting, Islam reflected the populist spirit of the Abrahamic faiths—that is, "a moral challenge to humanity to rise above its personal grudges and pettiness and to respond to God by affirming belief in God's plan for [all of] humanity and working for its ultimate realization." Islam represented an activist ideology bent on creating a social-political order. There was much more here than merely a new sense of personal piety. The basic mission was to translate Islamic revelation into new law and polity. Therefore, coercive power, where necessary, could not be rejected.

While the new righteous order had to be attained primarily by a divinely guided appeal to conscience, there were times when the "rejection of faith became a threat to the corporate well-being of the

society and the cause of corruption on earth." Under those circumstances the Qur'an legitimized the use of force through the instrumen-
tality of jihad "as a prescriptive measure to arrest the harm caused to
the people at large and to redress the wrongs suffered by the weak at
the hands of those who perpetrated immoral conduct to defeat the
divine purposes on earth."

The Qur'an affirms that most armed struggles are reprehensible in
that they endanger the human order and human well-being. War may
legitimately be waged only with religious authorization. It must be
sanctioned by the Prophet or his successor. Moreover, it must have
religious-moral goals and must have the elimination of corruption as
its principal purpose.

In Islam, true peace is not simply the absence of war but the
achievement of justice, according to Sachedina. For true peace to be
attained, oppressive conditions must be removed, and sometimes this
goal can only be accomplished through violence. Islam views humanity as caught up in "the midst of contradictory forces of 'light' and
'darkness,' 'guidance' and 'misguidance,' 'justice' and 'injustice.' " Life
is an unending moral struggle for the creation of a just society on earth.
The emphasis on justice, equality among people, and the continuous
struggle to uproot corruption and oppression, by force if necessary,
means that Islam has no place for pacifism, if pacifism rejects all forms
of violence and opposes all war and armed hostility.

Although Islamic thought permits the use of force, Islam does seek
to exhaust all peaceful means to resolve conflict before resorting to
violence. Moreover, "quietism, which has been a strategy for survival
in minority communities with the hope of regrouping and reasserting
one's ideals of justice, was a legitimate posture in Islam from its early
history." Quietism or pragmatic pacifism is sometimes justified as the
prudential postponement of adopting offensive measures when the
probability of success is outweighed by the likelihood of destruction
and suffering. Quietism can be a temporary but strategic tactic adopted in the ongoing struggle to realize the ideal Islamic polity.

Divinely sanctioned Islamic leadership is central to the issue of violence, in Sachedina's view. Without widely acknowledged and legitimate leadership, there is no one in the Islamic community to interpret
revelation and to lead the way to create an Islamic public order.

"Religious leadership is the single most important issue that has divided the community and has provoked debates about the justification of engaging in religiously sanctioned violence to establish or dethrone it." A quietist approach has often been adopted because of a failure to agree on who is to lead the struggle to promote justice. A leadership struggle can lead to disruption and strife or even civil war, which in turn can precipitate major schisms within the community. Fear of such conflict often prompts Muslims to adopt quietist passivity. According to quietist thought, sinful rule and tyrannical government are not the greatest evils; chaos and disunity are.

Islamic revelation acknowledges that human volition frequently frustrates the divine plan.

> It points out ways in which those who reject the faith and its involvement in the moral realm conspire to defeat the divine purposes. To meet this challenge to the divine order, force, even armed struggle (*jihad*), is sanctioned as a legitimate defensive measure to subdue those who are hostile to the establishment of justice. However, at no time is human life to be destroyed without justification because the Qur'an commands time and again: "Slay not the life that God has made sacred." [Surah 6:152] Precisely at this point in the divine plan for humanity the role of the Prophet or the religious leader as the interpreter of the divine will becomes indispensable.

Without such a divinely guided leader, humanity has only reason, and that is an inadequate resource for discerning God's purposes. "Islam is both a critical assessment of human society and a program of action, whether leading to a quietist authoritarianism or an activist radicalism, as the situation may require, to realize God's will on earth to the fullest extent possible."

Thus, Islam, in attempting to create a just and equitable society on earth, grants no place to absolute or principled pacifism. Violence may be undesirable, but it is sometimes necessary, as Muhammad's own repeated resort to arms in Medina showed. Persuasion is always the first step in promoting the good, but if it fails, force may be required.

According to Sachedina, some minorities, especially those associated with the Sufi tradition, dissent from the conventional Islamic attitude toward nonviolence. For example, certain opposition communities in Egypt, Sudan, Iran, and elsewhere adopt nonviolence, seeking to challenge oppressive governments through negotiation rather than violence.

In response to Sachedina and drawing on a different set of assumptions, Professor Michael Nagler of the University of California at Berkeley noted that despite the many differences among Christianity, Judaism, and Islam in regard to violence, "the impression I am left with is the impressive fundamental similarity among the people of the Book." They all confront the paradox posed by two fundamental tenets of all three of these faiths. The Qur'an says, "Take not the life which I have given, for it is sacred." Side by side with this injunction is the necessity to fight in self-defense and even more to fight for justice ("Persecution is worse than slaughter" [Surah 2:191]). "As long as you believe that nonviolence is not mighty or effective, you cannot be both nonviolent and just. That God asks humanity both to eschew violence and to fight for justice—particularly normative in Islam—puts us in an impossible dilemma, a real moral quagmire."

At present, Islam is unfortunately being stereotyped as fundamentalist, threatening, and deeply violent. For Nagler, such stereotypes prevent people from seeing how basic nonviolence is to Islam. By identifying the nonviolent currents in Islam, we can do "the most effective thing possible to dispel that dangerous and oppressive stereotype." Like Jews, many Muslims reject nonviolence not so much because it is inconsistent with the tenets of their faith, but because they view it as an ineffective strategy in the pursuit of justice.

Nagler urged that one avoid identifying nonviolence with merely the absence of violence and hence with powerlessness. Gandhi was able to adapt nonviolence to the most unlikely situations and use it against apparently overwhelming power, often with impressive success. Gandhi grasped that "alongside a handful of situations in which we can see the force of persuasion toward justice operating, what Mirsky calls the 'nonviolent moment,' are an infinite set of moments in which nonviolence is immanent and we can release its operations if we make ourselves the right instruments to do so."

Nagler contended that the most spectacular demonstration of nonviolent power the world has seen was orchestrated and led by Khan Abdul Ghaffar Khan, the so-called Frontier Gandhi who has also been called a "nonviolent soldier of Islam." Khan, a Pathan leader, came under Gandhi's direct influence in the 1920s and inspired nonviolent Muslim volunteers, the Khudai Khidmatgars, or Servants of God, to dogged resistance under intense provocation. "The historical example of a trained, uniformed army of brave, formerly violent people resisting oppression without weapons or violence—and the Pathans knew how to use both—is an extremely important factor today in the arguments for the creation of volunteer nonviolent international peace brigades.... If Khan's example had been actively followed, the Pathans and others could have saved Afghanistan from the Soviets; more to the point, we could be saving Bosnia-Hercegovina right now."

This important example of nonviolent action emerged in a distinctly Islamic context, Nagler pointed out, and a context that was quite orthodox. Khan stated, "There is nothing surprising in a Muslim or a Pathan like me subscribing to the creed of nonviolence. It is not a new creed. It was followed fourteen hundred years ago by the Prophet all the time he was in Mecca, and it has since been followed by all those who wanted to throw off an oppressor's yoke. But we had so far forgotten it and when Gandhi placed it before us, we thought he was sponsoring a novel creed." Nonviolence has been neglected as a means of confronting war, Nagler contended, and it was mainly a Muslim who demonstrated its feasibility on a significant scale.

Mainstream Islam does not embrace nonviolence, Nagler noted, but there is nothing in Islam that is inconsistent with nonviolence or that should prohibit the development of nonviolent movements within Islam. Many Islamic traditions support nonviolence. For instance, a Hadith from the prestigious *Sahih Bukhari* states: "Help your brother whether he is an aggressor or a victim of aggression." When the Prophet is asked how to help the aggressor, he replies, "by doing your best to stop him from aggression." Surah 5:35 states: "If anyone takes a life, it is as though he slays all mankind. And if anyone saved a life, it would be as if he saved the life of the whole people."

Commending Professor Sachedina for his presentation on Islam and nonviolence, Kelsay asserted that analysts who proclaim that Islam is a religion of peace and has nothing to do with war mislead us and keep us from the wisdom we might attain from attending to the Islamic tradition's reflections on the use of force. It is essential to evaluate nonviolence in terms of Islam's overall goal: the establishment of a just social reality. "The question is not: Does Islam provide support for nonviolence? The issue is rather: when, where and how do nonviolent strategies serve the goal of establishing and maintaining this social reality which Islam is after?"

There are times when Muslims opt for various forms of nonviolence, Kelsay said. The first is when considerations of proportionality and probable success indicate that resort to force would backfire on the community and do more harm than good. The second is when a dispute exists about whether there is a leader with the legitimate authority to decide to go to war. While these two situations are well known and documented in the history of Islam, there is a third in which nonviolence would be a useful strategy: Active nonviolence can be adopted to promote justice. Although this option is not often considered within Islam, Kelsay said, "It seems to me that there might be a warrant in particular situations for Muslims to adopt a kind of pragmatic active strategy of nonviolent resistance."

Kelsay referred to Wilfred Cantwell Smith's statement that Islam views history as a field of struggle. The struggle is aimed at establishing a political world in which divinely sanctioned values are encouraged and in some cases enforced. Kelsay pointed out that Muslims will continue to debate their choices within concrete social contexts, in which the positive value of peace must be weighed against the negative reality of injustice, and that it must be determined how justice can most effectively be promoted in particular situations.

In an effort to broaden the scope of the discussion of Islam and nonviolence, Professor Mumtaz Ahmad of Hampton University noted that Sufis accord high priority to conquest of self. Sufi communities emphasize the Prophet's teaching that one's battle with oneself is more difficult and more compelling than jihad against the enemies of Islam. Sufis adopt quietism not as an act of despair, disgust, or defeatism, but as a positive and activist approach to the promotion of justice through purification of self.

Ahmad also cited examples of active nonviolent resistance by Islamic communities. The founder of the Khudai Khidmatgar movement, in confronting British colonialism in India, delegitimized violence on the basis of his interpretation of Islamic texts and theology. In another instance, the founder of the Ahmadiya movement declared that jihad had been abolished and was no longer relevant. Nonviolent resistance has also been employed by some contemporary Islamist movements in Nigeria, Egypt, and Pakistan.

Another tradition within Islam is based on the Prophet's statement that when an injustice occurs, there is warrant to prevent or correct it by force, but if that cannot be done, the tongue may be used. As Ahmad pointed out, promoting justice with the tongue and the heart is usually a weaker approach than promoting justice through force. But the tongue and the heart are both legitimate alternatives to violence, particularly when the community concludes that violence cannot be effective or will even be counterproductive. The Tabligh movement in contemporary Islam follows this approach to Islamic change.

Responding to these various comments, Professor Sachedina said that just as the discussion of the role of nonviolence in Judaism generated conflicting interpretations of Jewish texts, so different Islamic interpreters draw contrasting conclusions from Islamic texts. There is more than one way to interpret the sources. While some interpreters defend Islamic nonviolence, the Shi'ites of south Lebanon, for example, dwell on the importance of violence, and they are able to invoke several traditions of the Prophet and of the imams to defend their position.

Still, if Muslims are like Christians and Jews in drawing different lessons about nonviolence from their traditions, they are distinctive in one important way. Whichever position they take, Muslims tend, particularly in the Middle East, to emphasize the impact of religion on public policy and on questions of war and peace in a way that sets them apart.

5

Comparison of Three Faith Traditions

How do the three faiths compare in their disposition toward pacifism and nonviolence? In the fourth paper of the conference, Professor J. Patout Burns of Washington University in St. Louis noted that in Christianity and Islam a principled pacifism is upheld by a determined minority that also asserts that the type of divine intervention in human history that established the religion can be anticipated in the future. The course of history, and in particular the state of the faithful community, is in God's hands; it need not be defended by human coercive force. Muslim pacifists believe that arms might be taken up only under a divine mandate, which they expect at the end of time. Christian pacifists believe that the revelation of God's will in the life and teaching of Jesus Christ forever excludes such a recourse to coercive violence. Judaism, unlike the traditions deriving from it, no longer anticipates a particular divine mandate that would make a war either obligatory or forbidden.

Within each of these religious traditions, Burns continued, well-established positions contradict an absolute or principled pacifism. The majority positions define certain values that must be established and protected, even through recourse to violence. Thus Judaism insists on the continued existence of the people itself; Islam requires not only the protection of the community and its freedom of religious practice, but also the establishment of a just society; Christianity grants a right of self-defense and imposes an obligation to protect the neighbor, and these principles form the foundation for its just war theory.

Yet the values that justify and even require warfare in each tradition, Burns asserted, can also serve as the foundation for a pragmatic pacifism that actually forbids the recourse to arms in certain situations. If violence can reasonably be expected to undermine the objectives that would be achieved through force, then, to protest these values, war must be renounced. Thus Jews in a minority status in the Diaspora have adopted submission and passive resistance as more likely than violence to secure the safety of the people. Muslims have tolerated unjust government to avoid the breakdown of the community in civil strife and to secure the freedom of religious practice under a western imperial power. They have also refused to acknowledge an institutional authority capable of issuing the call to arms in God's name. The Christian just war sets conditions and defines situations in which recourse to arms is unjustified and therefore forbidden.

Burns also observed that Christianity and Islam actually promote a principled pacifism by requiring the renunciation of violence among certain classes of the faithful. Christian monks and most clergy are expected to abstain from bloodshed and coercion, even when these are recognized as appropriate for others. The Muslim orders promote similar commitments among their members. Within Judaism as well, the anticipation of the Messianic Age may serve as the foundation for a principled nonviolence. This symbolic pacifism establishes the ideal toward which each faith tradition exhorts its adherents.

Finally, Burns noted that the religious category of obligatory warfare, originally operative in each of these traditions but generally abandoned by them, has now been taken up by the secular states. The modern ideological war is fought to achieve a value that transcends national self-interest, that grants the adversary no rights, and that need not be winnable. The violence and destruction of such wars have in fact been limited only by the energies and resources of the opponents. This new theory of ideological warfare deserves to be unmasked as a reversion, in an alternative religious system, to the holy war that has been generally renounced by both the principled and pragmatic pacifism of Judaism, Christianity, and Islam.

Building on Burns's argument, Langan identified the centrality of the concept of power to a discussion of pacifism. All three Abrahamic faiths recognize God as the center of power. A commitment to nonviolence entails some tension around the notion of power. These faiths believe that power comes from God, yet military might is able to dominate most forms of power. The transformation of political power is comparatively easy in some societies at some times, while in others it is incredibly hard. Pacifism entails a renunciation of a particular form of power, military power.

A different view of power in relation to pacifism was offered by Joe Volk of the Friends Committee on National Legislation. According to Volk, pacifism is an affirmation rather than a renunciation of power. People committed to nonviolence are usually those who believe there is a transcending power with whom they are working. They are in partnership with that sacred power. Of course, those committed to military force often feel the same way. Volk said:

> I often hear people say that when everything else has failed, then we must resort to the option of last resort—war. The implication is that war should be used because it will succeed. Belief that war will succeed is not a statement of fact, but rather a faith statement. I think it is a religious statement that implies that the god whose power comes from love is a weak god. And when times get rough, when we are in trouble, when world order has collapsed and we are in chaos, that is the time to turn to another god. The god of death is the god that can help us put things back in order. And we will work with that god until we get things back in place. This is a religious commitment. It is not Jewish, or Christian, or Islamic. The pacifist does not believe in the promise of death to deliver world order and security, but the person who takes up arms does, or gives in to others who do.

Taking exception to these claims, Hittinger asserted that it does not fall to human beings to cure the human heart in any direct way. That task belongs to God. Human beings may control only exterior acts. As Aristotle contended, justice is the one thing that can be accomplished without virtue because it has to do with the external, not internal, matters. Even a reprobate can do justice. "When we kill in order to achieve certain kinds of justice, we are not claiming to cure the human heart. We are not claiming that kind of power." People who expect to change the human heart through nonviolent politics are close to challenging divine prerogatives.

6

Peaceforce: A Nonviolent Strategy for Intervention

How can pacifism and nonviolence promote peace in situations of international conflict? What alternative approaches might be adopted to traditional forms of diplomacy, military intervention, and peace-keeping?

In the final paper of the conference, Professor John Paul Lederach of Eastern Mennonite College and of the Mennonite Central Committee's International Conciliation Service proposed a concrete agenda to create an infrastructure for peace and advocated the creation of an international Peaceforce.

Lederach asserted that the realities of current conflicts, most of which are internal rather than international, illustrate the limitations and inadequacies of traditional "statist diplomacy." Traditional assumptions of the following sort, on which international diplomacy has been built, are increasingly being challenged.

1. Groups in conflict operate by defined hierarchies of power, making authoritative representation in decision making and negotiations possible.

2. Political, cultural, and social power bases are dependent on military power, making the achievement of a cease-fire equivalent to terminating a conflict.

3. Conflicts are primarily motivated and sustained by substantive interests, historically defined as national interests.

4. Solutions are best sought by pragmatic compromise of interests.

Peacemaking is traditionally seen as trickling down from the top level to the lower levels of society. The top level is given prominence and importance, and the lower levels are generally neglected or treated as peripheral and incidental to success. This misplaced emphasis derives from statist and diplomatic biases toward dealing primarily with hierarchies of political or military structures, according to Lederach.

Lederach presented an analytic scheme with three levels of intervention, including actors and their respective activities (see figure). On one side are those directly involved in the conflict; on the other are those involved in peacemaking efforts. In Lederach's analysis, level 1 involves highly visible political and military leaders, who are usually locked into bargaining positions. "Peacemaking and conflict resolution activities are aimed at achieving ceasefires via high level negotiations between representative leaders, often brokered by high profile mediation efforts involving eminent personalities." Diplomatic processes at this level entail a very limited number of people assumed to be representative of large numbers, to be acting in their best interest, and to be capable of delivering their constituents.

> Level 2 involves a "middle range" set of actors, more numerous and connected to multiple sectors and regions. These are often significant religious, ethnic, sectoral leaders, as well as key NGO [nongovernmental organization], PVO [private voluntary organization],and middle level military people, activists, and government officials. Particularly in protracted conflicts with intense religious or ethnic divisions, these leaders may represent regional and/or factional interests that affect given geographic areas, and are often in contact with and influenced, but may or may not feel bound by decisions made at the highest level. They are also in more direct contact with day to day operations on the ground in their respective areas. Peacemaking activities at this level could involve the creation of a broader participation in the peace process and establishing an infrastructure and capacity for dispute resolution within the setting across the lines of conflict. These may involve workshops addressing immediate decisionmaking issues, conflict resolution training, development of peace commissions for dealing with ethnic issues in a given region, or even the formation of mediation or consultant teams built from within the context.

The grassroots level, according to Lederach, involves key local actors such as indigenous NGOs; community developers; women's

Three Types of Actors in the Affected Population and Peacemaking Focuses

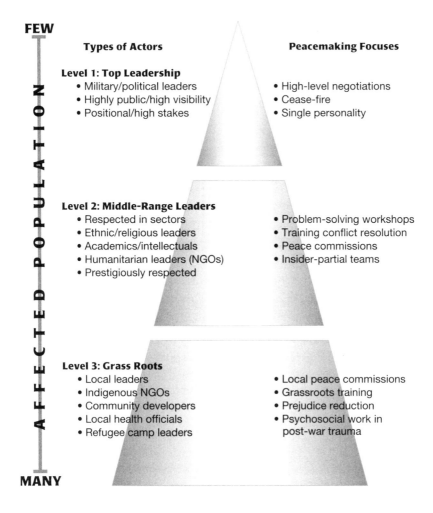

FEW

AFFECTED POPULATION

Types of Actors

Peacemaking Focuses

Level 1: Top Leadership
- Military/political leaders
- Highly public/high visibility
- Positional/high stakes

- High-level negotiations
- Cease-fire
- Single personality

Level 2: Middle-Range Leaders
- Respected in sectors
- Ethnic/religious leaders
- Academics/intellectuals
- Humanitarian leaders (NGOs)
- Prestigiously respected

- Problem-solving workshops
- Training conflict resolution
- Peace commissions
- Insider-partial teams

Level 3: Grass Roots
- Local leaders
- Indigenous NGOs
- Community developers
- Local health officials
- Refugee camp leaders

- Local peace commissions
- Grassroots training
- Prejudice reduction
- Psychosocial work in post-war trauma

MANY

associations; local religious, health, municipal, and business leaders; and those involved in refugee camps. "Peacemaking activities here could involve a broad set of efforts from training to the formation of peace commissions that negotiate daily issues and deal with the multiplicity of conflicts taking place at local levels." Lederach continued:

> I would argue that contemporary conflict calls for the development of a framework for sustainable transformation that builds across the

population and in many instances from the bottom-up or the middle-out. "Transformation" refers to movement and change. In the context of conflict it suggests movement away from relationships dominated by fear, animosity and threat and toward those dominated by understanding, cooperation and mutual respect. This includes the traditional concepts of ceasefires and top level negotiations, but goes beyond, encompassing the relational concept of reconciliation. "Sustainability" suggests the concern not only for how to initiate such movement but how to create a proactive process capable of regenerating itself over time. As a framework, sustainable transformation suggests the need to establish an infrastructure for peace within a setting, the promotion of citizen-based initiatives as legitimate and necessary at various levels, a long term commitment to relationship building and a willingness to seek out and root peace activities in the cultural context of the conflict.

Peacemaking based on the notion of sustainable transformation is rooted in Lederach's Anabaptist faith and "the belief that the Kingdom of God emerges not by the pursuit nor usurpation of power from on high, even for the best of reasons, but rather through the transformation of people and relationships from below." He explained that his position is not based on specific biblical verses that mandate nonviolence, but rather

> on a world view of how God is present and acts in history and how we, as followers and disciples of Christ, are part of that presence. It is the story of the incarnation, of God who had all power and resources at hand, yet chose to bring about change through sacrifice and weakness, by becoming one of us, by assuming a position of weakness and by working from the bottom up. It is the story of the formation of a community of disparate and even antagonistic members who became the pillars and prophets of a movement that changed the world. It is the story of living by alternative values in the face of overwhelming odds. . . . This theology looks at contemporary conflict and believes in the foolishness that change is possible, that it will happen both through individuals and structures, that it will be sustained not by a Moses but by a movement of members willing to risk their own lives for the envisioned change and one that ultimately finds its sustenance in the grace and guiding of God's spirit. It is based upon Christ moving between and connecting enemy peoples.

Given this theological and conceptual framework, Lederach advocated a strategy for peacemaking that assumes peace will not trickle down from the top. Peacemaking must provide for involvement of all levels of society and create linkages among these levels and between the groups in conflict. An infrastructure for peace is primarily based on people. Citizen-based peacemaking of this kind is built largely on middle-range actors. These actors are generally deeply involved in contemporary conflicts, and they often enjoy the trust of both those at the top and those at the grass roots. If they can grasp their roles as peacemakers and create bridges to counterparts across the lines of conflict, they can serve as valuable brokers for peace. Peacemaking depends on the use of local resources; the potential for conflict resolution needs to be discovered in each setting. "From understanding and making use of the role of elders in Somalia, to the ironic role of paramilitary networks in Northern Ireland, to the modalities of how *confianza* is used and built in Nicaragua, peacemaking must identify and build on local, contextual resources if long-term transformation is desired."

Religious institutions, particularly churches, can play a key role in contextualized peacemaking, Lederach asserted. From the Philippines to the Balkans, from Mozambique to El Salvador, religious actors are centrally involved in situations of conflict. While church members are often divided and polarized, a shared faith cuts across the lines of conflict and can be used as a basis for reconciliation. Moreover, "the primary arena of church activity and faith—that of spiritual, emotional, and relational well-being of people—lies at the heart of contemporary conflict." Insofar as the church and other religious institutions are promoting reconciliation, they can be at the center of conflict transformation.

As a concrete agenda to create an infrastructure and a constituency for peace, Lederach advocated the following:

1. Promote workshops on reconciliation across religious traditions and affiliations, at which people are engaged to seek resources from their own faith traditions as responses to the conflict and to create an active form of ecumenism that encourages conciliation, the reduction of prejudice, and peacemaking.

2. Promote training in conflict resolution and mediation, especially at middle and grassroots levels, with a focus on uncovering and building on local resources for peacemaking. Where possible, such training should involve participants from both sides of the conflict.

3. Encourage and support teams for carrying out local and regional mediation and serving as key consultants to higher level negotiations.

4. Encourage the media to create film or radio projects aimed at disseminating peace efforts at middle and grassroots levels to broaden the sense of activity and actors in the process.

5. Broaden programs of NGOs, PVOs, and government agencies to link conciliation and peacemaking activities with more traditional arenas of relief and development.

Beyond this, Lederach argued for the development of nonviolent peacekeeping operations. He expressed doubt about the effectiveness and moral justification of international military intervention in contemporary conflict. As a short-term measure, such intervention may adversely affect and impede progress toward long-term resolution of conflict. The danger becomes greater when military intervention for humanitarian purposes is undertaken without full approval of the parties to the conflict, when all actors and goals become subordinate to military effectiveness, or when local factions exploit intervention to support or undermine one or another of the parties in conflict.

In contrast to the negative implications of military intervention, Lederach argued that nonviolence has a positive value in international peacekeeping. "Ours is the task of being faithful to God's redemptive project that seeks peace and pursues it and to envision, articulate and implement nonviolent alternatives that, consistent with this project, are better alternatives for dealing with the violence and atrocities of contemporary conflict than increased militarization."

Lederach asserted that the development of what he calls a "Peaceforce" could be as effective as militarized peacekeeping in the short term and that it would prove far more effective than the military approach over the long term. The development of a Peaceforce would require a commitment to creating a standing international corps of people trained in nonviolence, riot control, observation, conciliation, and negotiation. "It is my belief that where deployed on a large scale, with international legitimacy and rigorous nonviolent discipline, such a body could effectively move to protect vulnerable populations, assure the delivery of aid, monitor and promote cease-fires and safe-havens." Where pacifism is most needed, Lederach continued, is in the worst of the "messes contemporary conflict offers us, and it should be no more or less risky for us who choose to be present than for those who carry the gun." A Peaceforce of 30,000 sent to war-torn Somalia or Bosnia could be more effective in promoting peace than the armed peacekeepers who have been sent there.

Getting down to specifics, Lederach proposed the creation of an international Peaceforce, committed to nonviolence, under UN auspices. The Peaceforce would number 250,000 by the year 2000 and be composed of well-trained, cross-national, and self-sufficient units. The members would be paid and would enlist for five-year assignments following a full year of training. The Peaceforce would accompany relief deliveries in settings of armed conflict, provide protection to vulnerable populations, and secure and monitor cease-fires while negotiations are pursued and implemented. Peacekeeping training centers could be established—one each in Africa, Asia, Latin America, North America, and Europe. Funding for the Peaceforce would come from a variety of sources, including a levy on each UN member state of 1 percent of its annual military budget.

In commending Lederach's paper, Professor Susan Brooks Thistlethwaite of Chicago Theological Seminary noted the compatability between Lederach's notion of sustainable transformation and several principles of just peace as articulated by the United Church of Christ. Both formulations highlight the structural dimensions of violence and nonviolence, both entail long-term commitment, and both emphasize the international character of peacemaking. For instance, Principle 10 of the Just Peace Declaration states that "unexpected initiatives of friendship and reconciliation can transform interpersonal and international relationships and are essential to restoring community." Principle 9 states that "international structures of friendship, justice and common security from violence are necessary and possible at this point in history in order to eliminate the institution of war and move toward a Just Peace." She also remarked that Lederach's Peaceforce proposal seemed to be modeled on Witness for Peace and other attempts to be actively present and nonviolent in Central America, and she asserted that "Peaceforce is a welcome addition to the lexicon of peacemaking."

An omission in Lederach's presentation, according to Thistlethwaite, was that it did not challenge "the consciousness of those who would be a force for peace on the subject of human rights abuses of women and its relation to the culture of militarism." Among the most offensive of such abuses has been the systemic gender-based torture of women in the Balkans through rape and forced impregnation. She argued that unless and until there is a changed consciousness among peace activists, "transformational strategies will leave out half the human race." Peacemakers need to name violence against women as wrong, and they have to place the blame clearly on the perpetrators. A Peaceforce would need to be trained to be sensitive to and to respond supportively to cases of violence against women.

7

How Can Nonviolence Address International Conflict?

A Discussion

Not surprisingly, the conference papers and responses generated considerable discussion about how nonviolence could be used in current conflicts around the globe, including Israel, Somalia, and Bosnia.

Citing the case of the Intifada in Israel, Mordechai Bar-On, former member of the Knesset in Israel and former chief education officer for the Israeli army, asserted that young Palestinians transformed the Israeli political equation through the use of nonviolent resistance. They changed the terms of the debate and opened up the possibility for the Middle East peace talks, all by turning the other cheek and confronting Israeli authorities for the most part nonviolently. Peace is a possibility only when each side in a conflict stops generating hatred for the opposing side. As chief education officer in the Israeli army, Bar-On pushed the idea that hatred of the enemy is a sign and source of weakness rather than strength, and it delays the coming of peace.

Some advocate nonviolence because of perceived inadequacies of the military alternative. Volk noted the case of Somalia and stated that the "advocacy of military intervention [Operation Restore Hope and UNOSOM II] degenerated into a logic not of humanitarian service but of war." He contended that military intervention there has not benefited the Somali people. In the case of Iraq, military intervention, justified by just war criteria, countered Iraq's aggression against Kuwait.

"But has it worked out? Has it fixed the situation and at what cost?" Volk contended that just war theory was originally used to justify covert assistance to Saddam Hussein, on the basis of the erroneous belief that providing military assistance to Saddam Hussein would make the world safer, particularly from Iran. Volk argued that it is incumbent upon the advocates of military intervention not merely to invoke just war theory, but also to engage in a moral discourse that considers all the consequences of military action.

Although the complex and devastating civil war among Muslims, Croats, and Serbs in Bosnia has presented the most troubling case of all, both for proponents of military and nonviolent intervention, Nagler asserted that the only approach with any chance of promoting peace there would be a nonviolent, volunteer "army." A peace group of 500 members successfully entered Sarajevo in December 1992 to offer humanitarian aid and refused to accept the protection of the UN peace-keeping forces. Nagler contended that the only way to stop the violence in Bosnia is to "break the mystique, the mental outlook to which people involved in violent conflicts always succumb, that of 'polar otherness.'" Conflicts are sustained because those in the conflict regard their enemies as inhuman, but this mental construct can be shattered when third parties are prepared to step in and risk their lives to save those engaged in conflict. The effectiveness of such intervention comes largely from its shock value, forcing the enemies to reassess the harm they are perpetuating. When someone provides humanitarian care to the injured and refugees of Bosnia, Nagler pointed out, that can change the thinking of the Serbian infantrymen who up to that point probably do not care about the suffering of the people they are attacking.

One reason that peace groups are not able to organize effectively to intervene in situations of international conflict is that government and nongovernment funding organizations are not prepared to provide financial support. Mubarak Awad of Nonviolence International pointed out that while weapons of war are always available, instruments of peace are not.

Those who favor military power as the solution to international conflicts neglect soul force, or spiritual force, commented Richard Deats of the Fellowship of Reconciliation. The spiritual power of nonviolence is effective not only when it confronts British colonial authorities in India or sheriffs in the southern United States. "Solidarity came face to face with a totalitarian government in Poland and as a consequence Polish authorities declared martial law and outlawed Solidarity. But as they were pushed underground, Solidarity members and other Poles decided to live as if they were free. And in living as if they were free, they began to discover that they were free. Over a period of years they overthrew the totalitarian power that had conquered them." Deats said that nonviolence represents an alternative vision of history and of reality that helps us discover the true power that lies within us. Enormous power is released when we see human life as sacred and treat the enemy as sacred, unlocking a new way of dealing with history.

Drawing on a different set of assumptions, Land contended that in the case of Bosnia, multinational military intervention is justified and essential. He described the situation in Bosnia as "the most horrible thing that has happened in the world since the end of the holocaust." As with the nonresponse to the Holocaust, ethnic cleansing is under way in Bosnia without an adequate response from European and American governments. Land argued that effective military intervention in Bosnia is possible and that if action is not taken swiftly, rape and devastation will proceed unimpeded.

> When you look at the demography and ethnic makeup of the republics of the former Soviet Union, you realize that there are potential Bosnias on every horizon. If the international community shows that it is unwilling or unable to do anything about what is going on, then people who have these propensities and who have the power to do so are going to inflict unimaginable barbarities. I think we will look back on 1993 and Bosnia in the same way that we looked back on Ethiopia in 1935. We looked back at Ethiopia and saw that we lost an opportunity to have stopped something before it became much uglier.

While agreeing with Land's outrage over the obscene violence to which Bosnia is being subjected, Lintner wondered whether military intervention would actually reduce the level of violence. He also worried about singling out Bosnia for attention, when other areas of conflict in Africa and Asia warrant similar concern.

A major problem, Novak pointed out, is that we have not developed criteria or a consensus about when and where we should intervene when someone else is the victim. Novak contended that the best resource for developing such criteria is the just war theory as it has developed within Christianity, Judaism, and Islam. The problem with the nonviolent option is that pacifism tends toward ethical purity rather than toward the assumption of appropriate responsibility for those who are being victimized. Such ethical purity often is achieved at the expense of the victim. The religious traditions of the three Abrahamic faiths can offer resources for developing morally appropriate responses to international conflict, some of which may be nonviolent and some violent.

Taking exception to Bar-On's earlier reference to the Intifada as an illustration of the moral justification and effectiveness of nonviolence, Mirsky noted that the techniques adopted were not nonviolent. Simply put, stone throwing is a far cry from passive resistance. In addition, the methods adopted by the Intifada did not move the Israeli population to greater compassion or responsiveness to just and legitimate Palestinian aspirations, which should have been the principal purpose of the Intifada. Indeed the Israeli public, conditioned by its own experience of suffering, might well have been particularly receptive to the testimony of nonviolence.

Taking issue with Land's advocacy of multilateral intervention in Bosnia, Saperstein noted that that approach gives a veto to other states over a U.S. decision to intervene. The Jewish concept of the *Rodef*, which mandates intervention to protect innocent life, would not accept that the decision to intervene be made by consensus. If you act alone and you end up being in error, you will be held accountable; you have to act on your conscience even if sometimes that means standing alone.

Saperstein also recognized that the Christian just war principle of "probable success" may have inappropriately inhibited military intervention in Bosnia. "I think there is an argument to be made that force could have been used in a very limited manner that would have made it more costly for the Serbs to conduct their war. I do not know if it would have worked but sometimes you do things even not knowing that they are going to work." He noted that nonviolent actions are frequently taken without any assurance of success; action is taken on the basis of conscience. Sometimes military intervention may have to be initiated for the same reason, on the basis of conscience without assurance of success.

While the urge to intervene in Bosnia has been strong, Professor Alan Geyer of Wesley Theological Seminary contended that military authorities have been very reluctant to sanction military action. The reluctance of the United States and the European powers to intervene derives primarily from the strategic difficulties that would be encountered in pursuing military action there. He further noted that the U.S. religious community is deeply divided and largely immobilized about what government policy to advocate in relation to Bosnia. Ironically, some traditional pacifists have been among those advocating decisive intervention.

If nonviolent intervention is advocated for Bosnia, Ahmad said, the advocates need to articulate the specifics of their strategy. They need to indicate how a nonviolent approach will resolve the problem; how it will eliminate or at least reduce the agony, misery, and tragedy; and how it will generate a just and lasting solution. "It seems to me that to advocate a nonviolent, pacifist approach in Bosnia is similar to the advice given by Gandhi to the Jewish victims of Nazi persecution. That is, they should commit collective suicide."

Sachedina cited the case of the Shi'ites in southern Iraq. To speak to them of nonviolent resistance in their struggle against Saddam Hussein's regime is to elicit a charge that you are a compromiser and that you do not understand what is happening on the battlefield. Iraq's Shi'ites see themselves as being systematically destroyed while the world looks on. No one outside of Iraq is even thinking about the devastation under way in southern Iraq.

Offering more specific commentary on Lederach's presentation and his proposals for promoting reconciliation and for the deployment of a UN Peaceforce, Geyer suggested that an unarmed Peaceforce could offer a valuable complement to a lightly armed UN peacekeeping force. Without an armed force, however, what would happen when the unarmed Peaceforce fails to stop the fighting? In the same vein, Land asked what would happen when the Peaceforce is deployed in Bosnia and the Serbs start lobbing artillery shells into the middle of this peace brigade. Is not violence justified as a last resort after the peace brigade has been excluded, arrested, imprisoned, or killed and the war goes on? He continued: "Although I could not condone all aspects of the way World War II was fought or the events on the Allied side that led up to World War II, I am glad that the Allies resorted to violence because we live in a much better world today and we are speaking a different language. Some of us, by ethnic derivation, would not be here if violence was totally and completely renounced and Hitler had had his way with the world."

Echoing the point made by Land, Professor Dean Curry of Messiah College concurred that strategies of nonviolence can often be effective and that reconciliation should be promoted in situations of conflict, but then he asked how the international community should respond to those leaders and groups who have no interest in reconciliation. There are problems in the world, like Bosnia, that do not have solutions and that certainly are not going to be resolved by a Peaceforce whose purpose is reconciliation. He expressed doubt that Lederach had given adequate weight to the tragic quality of human nature and the pervasiveness of sin.

Responding to these comments, Lederach asserted that a Peaceforce should not be merely an adjunct to an armed UN peacekeeping force. "If there is always behind the Peaceforce the suspicion that this is only an experiment and as soon as it fails we are going to send in the real stuff, then I think the nonviolent approach of the Peaceforce is doomed to failure." In response to the point about last resort, Lederach said, "You ask what are you going to do in the last resort when the nonviolent approach does not work. I say that you have never given us the legitimate space to try nonviolence in a way that has the same level of backing that all military operations have enjoyed over the centuries."

Many of the difficulties encountered in previous efforts at peacemaking stem from their focus on the leadership and elites, continued Lederach. The best way to promote long-term peace is to work at the middle and grassroots levels to undercut the capacity of those on top to manipulate things and perpetuate conflict. We need to ask how we can work with people of faith at the middle levels to generate peaceful transformation. The ultimate justification for this approach comes not from strategic calculations but from faith that our imaginations and God's guidance will move us to a new path toward peace. God sent his son who died on behalf of his enemies, and that is the paradigm that motivates the nonviolent approach to peace.

Supporting Lederach, Lintner stated that the advocates of the last-resort criterion within the just war tradition fail to recognize that people with sufficient imagination and goodwill can always develop new nonviolent approaches. As a consequence, the notion of last resort has no real meaning, since there will always be new alternatives to violence that can be employed and tested. Moreover, those who advocate the use of violence often think in terms of the quick fix. The conflict in Yugoslavia has a history of at least 400 years. It is naive to think that a quick military solution can be achieved. Alternative means need to be identified to produce a structured peace.

Lintner commended Lederach's diagram of actors and peacemaking foci and suggested that it might help pacifists (most of whom come from the lower ranks of society) and just war advocates to engage in more effective dialogue. "Some people find pacifism very attractive because it is something that they can imagine they can do. 'I am not in power. I am not a ruler. I understand pacifism. I am not going to war.' Just war, on the other hand, is aimed not so much at what the average person does, but what the ruler does. The chart helps give a framework for more sustained dialogue about what pacifism really has to say to the ruler and what just war theory has to say to those at the bottom or in the middle levels."

On the other hand, Lintner worried that Lederach's approach might promote premature reconciliation. To push hard for reconciliation at the middle levels in a place like South Africa before a just formula had been negotiated would not serve the cause of peace and justice. Reconciliation ought not to be achieved at the expense of justice. In other places, government repression may not permit the kind of dialogue at the middle levels that the diagram implies is essential for transformative peace. Lintner also proposed that the Peaceforce be the creation of and under the control of the international religious community rather than the United Nations. The governments of the world represented in the United Nations would have little patience once its Peaceforce was attacked and would soon resort to violent alternatives. Religious bodies would have more patience and more commitment to nonviolence.

Citing surprising similarities between the approach Lederach proposed for achieving sustainable transformation and Operation Restore

Hope in Somalia, John Hirsch, who was deputy to Ambassador Robert Oakley and General Robert Johnston in Somalia, noted Operation Restore Hope's emphasis on engaging the grassroots and middle levels of society. Although the operation involved 30,000 U.S. troops, the underlying assumption was that insofar as possible, military engagement should be avoided. Operation Restore Hope encouraged women's groups, clan elders, and others at the middle and grassroots levels to be centrally involved in the peace process. This was not the kind of trickle-down approach that Lederach criticizes. Moreover, the achievement of a cease-fire was considered only an important first step, rather than the ultimate goal. Hirsch proposed that the best approach to international peacemaking would be to combine a lightly armed international peacekeeping operation with the kind of nonviolent Peaceforce Lederach proposed, the latter probably being organized by the religious community.

While reacting positively to many of the insights and proposals contained in Lederach's presentation, James Matlack of the American Friends Service Committee noted how far the world community is from being able to embrace Lederach's ideas. World leaders prefer quick and simple solutions to the world's problems, and the nonviolent way is rarely quick and simple. The military approach is seductive because at first glance it seems quick and simple. Although the Bush administration defended Operation Restore Hope as being quick, simple, and humanitarian, the international military presence in Somalia generated military clashes that subsequently plagued south Mogadishu.

Turning to Bosnia, Matlack noted that the American religious communities have reached a point of "gridlock," and he felt a kind of personal gridlock in regard to Bosnia. "There is no situation which I track which equals Bosnia in terms of the wrenching disparity between my attempt to be faithful to the values and convictions of my own approach and of the Quaker tradition and the kind of evil that is being perpetrated there, with the rapes and methodical daily shelling from the hills around Sarajevo." An appropriate response is elusive. If a Peaceforce had been available, the damage might have been less. But one danger of sending in a peace team committed to nonviolence is that if any members were killed or captured by local combatants, the

United States would send in a commando team from an aircraft carrier to pull them out. "The presence of the peace team would become a pretext for a new stage of U.S. armed intervention." Although the situation in Bosnia seems to have passed the point where a peace team might effectively intervene, Kosovo offers more promise. Matlack thought that a peace team deployed on the Kosovo border, in the towns, and in the rural areas where attacks were just beginning could serve as an effective deterrent.

Nagler objected to the way just war advocates put the advocates of nonviolence on the defensive. He made reference to a statement by Theodore Roszak that "people try nonviolence for a week and if it does not 'work' they go back to violence, which has not worked for centuries." There are cases in which nonviolence has been dramatically successful. Goa was wrested from the Portuguese in 1948 and 1949 when waves of nonviolent volunteers marched in to reclaim Goa for India despite harsh resistance. A comparative study was undertaken of the nonviolent Indian freedom struggle and the violent Algerian freedom effort. Many more casualties occurred in Algeria, and the quality of the freedom attained was markedly inferior to that in India. Although nonviolence is generally the preferred approach, Nagler conceded that there may be extreme situations in which force may be required, and Bosnia might be an example.

Citing historical examples to defend the use of force, Morrisey said that after the military broke the power of the Japanese and German tyrants, MacArthur and Marshall went to Japan and Germany, respectively, and changed the regimes peacefully. These cases demonstrate that it is possible to generate long-lasting, sustainable transformation using the military as a decisive component.

Speaking from her position as a pacifist and nonviolent activist, Shelley Douglass of Ground Zero Center for Nonviolent Action objected that the conversation was so predictable. When creative possibilities for nonviolent change are proposed, the discussion quickly moves to consider how soon violence can be introduced. There is a fixation on violence. Elise Boulding also objected that criticism of Lederach's ideas was posed in terms of worst imaginable cases. It would be productive to think more positively. For instance, an alternative future in which there is no reliance on military force should be imagined. We are so contaminated by the warrior-god image that we are generally unable to think about how a truly peaceful world might function. We need to strengthen our imaginations. Divine and human ingenuity are essential to the attainment of an ideal such as peace. The many little islands of "peace culture" in every society need to be nurtured in order to supplant the prevailing commitment to force. People need to discover that there are peaceable, creative, inventive, ingenious, fun, and playful ways of handling life's circumstances, including serious conflicts.

Awad emphasized the need to educate people for nonviolence. Training is essential if nonviolent approaches are to be successfully employed. Armies devote great resources to training, and similiar investments must be made in nonviolence.

Noting that most intrasocietal conflicts are historically rooted, Kelsay asked Lederach to address this aspect of the problem. Actors in situations of conflict tend to express themselves and their feelings through historical narratives that reinforce group solidarity and consciousness.

> It is a narrative that usually helps to legitimate one group's cause and to incriminate another group's behavior. It is further a narrative that over time has filtered its way into educational systems and into the public media. It usually has a religious dimension and sometimes religious authorities give sermons that invoke the history. It is used by political leaders to motivate their people and by military leaders to motivate the fighters. I think it is an interesting challenge to show how your model would address this kind of deeply entrenched group identity.

In response Lederach said that his awareness of the historical rootedness of these conflicts was one reason that he proposed nonviolent resolution and reconciliation. Quick answers and quick fixes, usually of a military character, will not work. Part of the task of building peace is to rewrite the historical narratives to which Kelsay refers. This rewriting must occur in settings where people interact in new ways. The problem-solving workshops devised by specialists like Herbert Kelman and Joseph Montville exemplify the creative learning situations that can assist with restructuring identities and resolving conflict.

Although his commitment to nonviolence derives fundamentally from his faith, Lederach said those who advocate nonviolence must be as thoughtful, creative, and practical as possible. Advocates of nonviolence have to generate concrete ideas that are so practical and compelling that others will be prepared to experiment with them as an alternative to the use of force. The peace-oriented religious community needs to articulate its vision and to gain as much space for it as possible. In response to a question about why he would want to encourage martyrdom by recruiting an unarmed Peaceforce, Lederach indicated that there are many people committed to serving the cause of peace and to meeting humanitarian needs around the world. Recruiting a Peaceforce is no more a call to martyrdom than recruiting armies, which goes largely unchallenged.

Expressing surprise at Lederach's proposed Peaceforce, Hittinger challenged the idea of using the state and an intergovernment organization like the United Nations to sponsor a project in nonviolence. "The modern state is uniquely ill-equipped to do this kind of good on the ground. The modern state does not know how to change people's hearts and minds. What happened to theology? What happened to the Christian witness? When you start doing infrastructure analysis and taxation, that is a far cry from my understanding of the anabaptist tradition. This is playing the role of Caesar without a gun." In response, Lederach conceded that to generate funds from taxation for a project in nonviolence is to diverge from traditional Mennonite thinking, but there is need for some "legitimate space," which can come from government involvement and support.

Another role for a Peaceforce, that of violence prevention, was proposed by Thistlethwaite. Rather than confining its activities to stopping violence and reconstruction after violence, a nonviolent team could be very effective, possibly more effective, by intervening when tensions are building and before violence has broken out. The Peaceforce could identity at-risk locations around the world and work to reduce tension, avoid violence, and achieve reconciliation.

Land asserted that some of the disagreement between the adherents to just war theory and to principled nonviolence relates to the Fall and to sin. Those who espouse just war theory generally are more pessimistic about human nature in its fallen state. Admittedly, nonviolent resistance can and must play a significant role in social change, and King's effectiveness in the civil rights movement demonstrates that.

King was able to force white Southerners to come face-to-face with the abject contradiction between what they said they believe and the way they were behaving toward people of color, without being able to put that aside and resort to violence to defend themselves. . . . But this did not happen in a vacuum. The violent fringe of white resistance in the South was held in check by military and police force. . . . When the 82nd Airborne went to Oxford, Mississippi, they did not have empty guns. And when those 300 U.S. Marshals went into Alabama, they did not have empty pistols.

8

Concluding Reflections

In reviewing the results of the conference, Professor John Howard Yoder of the University of Notre Dame suggested that the discussion had neglected some important topics. "We blind ourselves by concentrating so much on the debate between people of goodwill who think that sometimes you have to kill and people of goodwill who think that you should never kill. Those two positions are part of a scale; most people in the real world do not hold to either of these two positions."

Three other positions characterize the rest of the scale, according to Yoder. The first is "realism" or Machiavellianism, according to which people argue that the national interest is the most accountable way that a society can make its decisions regarding war and peace. Second is ideological warfare, embraced by fascists, communists, and some religious fanatics, who contend that people on the other side have no moral status; the enemy has no legitimacy in human history. Third, there is war used to prove the dignity or the manhood of the leader who makes decisions relating to war. "We have not talked about any of those three modes of thinking. Those are the way most people in Washington or in Moscow or in Rome or wherever else make decisions. My dignity as a man; our dignity as a transcendent cause that has a right to trample over other people; or the duty that everybody has to take care of Number One. Those are the three kinds of discourse that cause war, and we have not talked about any of them. I would suggest they feature on future agendas."

Several of the participants concluded that more common ground was evident than some aspects of the debate might have implied. Land, as an adherent of just war theory, conceded the significant limitations of the theory. Moreover, he recognized the very important role that should be granted to nonviolence in addressing international conflict. On the other side, one of the advocates of nonviolence acknowledged that under extreme circumstances, force is a legitimate last resort, a position that Gandhi adopted as well. Saperstein commented that "overwhelmingly we share a belief in all our religious traditions and among those on both sides of this debate that force must be avoided wherever possible." That means, he added, that there is a very large common agenda among people of faith that can and must be addressed collectively. "Moreover, it is incumbent upon those of us who argue that there can be a legitimate use of force to help avoid bringing about the circumstances where that would ever be necessary. And the fact is, we have not tried to do that, and trying it together seems to me to be the common agenda that we have."

Another shared responsibility is to identify what justice requires and then to advance it. According to Saperstein, the Talmud states that the sword enters the world because of justice delayed and justice denied, and as a consequence the religious voice must challenge the conscience of the nations and power structures of the world. "The prophetic experience as recounted in the Bible is fundamentally a nonviolent experience. The prophets did not take up arms and were willing to go to jail. And they were constantly willing to challenge the conscience of the leaders of the structures of power in that day. I think we, as a religious community, whatever we think about the question of the use of force, share the vast agenda we have inherited from the prophets, and we need to make it real in our own time." Moreover, all faiths share a responsibility not only to promote justice, but also to facilitate healing and reconciliation, to aid in the resolution of disputes that underlie conflict. Different faith groups can help each other think through the modalities and means of undertaking the task of moving beyond Pax to achieve Shalom—that is, to move beyond the mere absence of violence to the attainment of true peace with justice.

Noting what he senses to be a genuine softening of both just war and pacifist positions, Wink concluded that the issue is becoming more fluid, with both sides demonstrating a greater willingness to admit the weakness of their positions. He made reference to Land's criticism of aspects of the execution of World War II and of the degree to which power has corrupted the Israeli government after 1948:

> For my part, I have to admit that I really have no idea how in 1948 Israel could have protected itself nonviolently, and I really do not have much of an idea about what should be done in Bosnia. So there is a sense of coming together that I think reflects the fact that neither position is really able to answer all the questions. Bosnia, especially, has made all of us humbler. As a consequence, I see a degree of confluence as we move from more fixed moral stances to more pragmatic, nonideological positions.

Nonviolence, Wink continued, is a very powerful tool; it holds great promise for the recovery of humanity's spiritual dimension. But the advocates of nonviolence need just war theorists to criticize their "creative flights of imagination." Both advocates of just war and advocates of nonviolence are committed to reducing violence, and they need each other in order to think through these issues creatively and faithfully. Hopefully in the future the two groups can explore both their differences and the ground they share in a nonadversarial fashion.

Participant Biographies

Mumtaz Ahmad is an associate professor in political science at Hampton University in Virginia. He holds a Ph.D. in political science from the University of Chicago and has been a fellow at the Brookings Institution and at the International Institute of Islamic Thought. He is an associate editor of the *American Journal of Islamic Social Sciences*. His most recent book is *State, Politics, and Islam*.

Mubarak Awad is the president and founder of Nonviolence International, Washington, D.C., and is also a faculty member at the American University, where he teaches a graduate course, "Nonviolent Peacemaking." In 1985 he established the Palestinian Center for the Study of Nonviolence, in Jerusalem, which he operated until his expulsion from Israel in June 1988.

Mordechai Bar-On is a former member of the Israeli Knesset, leader of the Peace Now movement, and chief education officer in the Israel Defense Forces. He has written extensively on current political affairs and was a visiting professor at Hebrew University and a research fellow at the Ben Gurion Research Center at Sdeh-Boker. He has been active for several years on the board of the New Israel Fund and was elected president in June 1992. During 1992–93 he was a Peace Fellow at the United States Institute of Peace.

Elise Boulding, professor emerita at Dartmouth College and senior fellow in the Dickey Endowment, is project director of the International Peace Research Association in Boulder, Colorado. She served on the governing board of the United Nations University between 1980 and 1985 and is a former member of both the International Jury of the UNESCO Prize for Peace Education and the U.S. Commission for UNESCO. She was professor and chair at Dartmouth from 1978 until 1985 and has written many books including *The Underside of History: A View of Women through Time*. She has coauthored *Peace Culture and Society: Transnational Research and Dialogue* and *The Social System of the Planet Earth*.

J. Patout Burns is Thomas and Alberta White Professor of Christian Thought and director of the Center for Interreligious Dialogue at Washington University in St. Louis. He has also served in the Department of Religion at the University of Florida and the Department of Theology at Loyola University in Chicago. During his tenure, the Center for Interreligious Dialogue has sponsored both a conference on the ethics of waging war (January 1991) and one on quietism and pacifism (February 1993). With John Helgeland and Robert Daly, he has published a study of early Christian attitudes toward the Roman military.

Dean Curry is the chairman of the Department of History and Political Science and a professor of political science at Messiah College in Grantham, Pennsylvania. He is the author or editor of four books, including *A World without Tyranny: Christian Faith and International Politics*. A former John M. Olin Fellow, he serves on the board of the Peace, Freedom, and Security Studies Program of the National Association of Evangelicals.

Richard Deats is on the national staff of the Fellowship of Reconciliation (FOR), Nyack, New York, and has been with FOR since 1972. Deats is a Methodist minister, and he taught social ethics at Union Theological Seminary in the Philippines from 1959 to 1972. His books include *Nationalism and Christianity in the Philippines* and *Ambassador of Reconciliation: A Muriel Lester Reader*. He coedited *Active Nonviolence: A Way of Life, a Strategy for Change*.

Shelley Douglass was a cofounder and core community member of Ground Zero Center for Nonviolent Action from 1978 until 1989.

She is a graduate of the University of Wisconsin in Madison and has done graduate work at the Vancouver School of Theology in British Columbia. She has been involved in movements for peace and justice since the 1960s and currently lives with her husband in Birmingham, Alabama, where they have founded Mary's House, a Catholic Worker house of hospitality. She has written and spoken extensively on nonviolence.

Alan Geyer is professor of political ethics and ecumenics at Wesley Theological Seminary and is concurrently senior scholar at the Churches' Center for Theology and Public Policy. He is contributing editor to *Christian Century*, of which he was formerly editor, and he was formerly an editor of *Christianity and Crisis*. His most recent book, with Barbara Green, is *Lines in the Sand: Justice and the Gulf War*. He was president of the Society for Christian Ethics and has served on the governing boards of the National Council of Churches, the Carnegie Council on Ethics and International Affairs, the Society for Values in Higher Education, and Ohio Wesleyan University.

Naomi Goodman was president of the Jewish Peace Fellowship from 1972 until 1987 and is currently its secretary. She has been the honorary vice chairperson of the Fellowship for Reconciliation since 1988, has served on the advisory board of the Shalom Center since 1986 and on the executive committee of the International Fellowship of Reconciliation between 1974 and 1984. She is the coeditor of *The Challenge of Shalom: The Jewish Tradition of Peace and Justice* (forthcoming) and has written articles and book reviews for *Fellowship*, *IFOR Report*, *Shalom*, *New Directions for Women*, *Present Tense*, and other periodicals.

John Hirsch is a career foreign service officer with twenty-seven years of experience, including assignments in Israel, Pakistan, and Somalia and at the U.S. mission to the United Nations. He recently completed a three-year tour as consul general in Johannesburg, South Africa. During this time, he joined Ambassador Robert Oakley in Somalia from December 1992 to March 1993, serving as his deputy and as political adviser to General Robert Johnston. During the summer of 1993 he worked with Ambassador Oakley at the United States

Institute of Peace to produce a monograph on the implications of Operation Restore Hope for UN peacekeeping. He has a B.A. from Columbia University and an M.A. and Ph.D. from the University of Wisconsin.

Russell Hittinger is an associate professor in the School of Philosophy at the Catholic University of America. Since 1990 he has been a research fellow at the American Enterprise Institute in Washington, D.C. His books and articles have appeared in such places as Oxford University Press, the University of Notre Dame Press, the *Review of Metaphysics*, the *Review of Politics*, and the *International Philosophical Quarterly*. He is currently preparing, under National Endowment for the Humanities funding, an English edition of the entire *De Legibus* of Thomas Aquinas, along with a commentary on the work.

John Kelsay is associate professor of religion at Florida State University, where he teaches courses in ethics and Islamic studies. He coedited *Cross, Crescent, and Sword* and *Just War and Jihad*. His most recent book is *Islam and War: The Gulf Crisis and Beyond*.

Richard D. Land is the executive director-treasurer of the Christian Life Commission of the Southern Baptist Convention. He received his Th.M. from New Orleans Baptist Theological Seminary and his D.Phil. from Oxford University. He has taught extensively and has served as a minister since 1969. His publications include *II Corinthians Commentary* in the New American Commentary by Broadman Press, "Citizen Christians: Their Rights and Responsibilities," and *Baptist Confessional Statements: A People Identifying Themselves through the Enunciation of Their Faith*.

John Langan, S.J., is the Rose F. Kennedy Professor of Christian Ethics in the Kennedy Institute of Ethics at Georgetown University and senior fellow at the Woodstock Theological Center, where he has served since 1975. He holds a Ph.D. in philosophy from the University of Michigan. He entered the Society of Jesus in 1957 and was ordained to the priesthood in Detroit in 1972. His many essays and articles have appeared in a wide variety of books and journals; with William O'Brien he edited *The Nuclear Dilemma and the Just War Tradition*, and with Alfred Hennelly, S.J., he edited *Human Rights in the Americas: The Struggle for Consensus.* He has acted as a consultant and expert on ethics for the Chemical Bank and the U.S. Navy Corps of Chaplains.

John Paul Lederach is an associate professor of sociology at Eastern Mennonite College and director of International Conciliation Service, Mennonite Central Committee, in Harrisonburg, Virginia. He received his Ph.D. from the University of Colorado and has extensive experience in mediation, training, and dispute resolution. His publications include: *Els anomenats pacifistes: La no-violència a l'estat espanyol*, and "The Conflict in Nicaragua's Atlantic Coast" in *War and Peacemaking: Essays in Conflict and Change.* He is currently a consultant to the Somali Peace and Consultation Committee.

Jay Lintner is director of the Washington Office for the United Church of Christ's Office for Church in Society. In 1991 he played an active role in developing the church's response to the Gulf War and to the Civil Rights Act of 1991. He holds an M.Div. and D.D. from Chicago Theological Seminary. His publications include *Peace Futuring*, *Empowering the Church in Society*, *The United Church of Christ Social Policy*, and "God's Unbroken Covenant with the Jews" (in *New Conversations*).

David Little is senior scholar in religion, ethics, and human rights at the United States Institute of Peace. He is also director of the Institute's Working Group on Religion, Ideology, and Peace, which is currently conducting a two-year study of religion, nationalism, and intolerance. He was formerly professor of religious studies at the University of Virginia and has also taught at Harvard and Yale Divinity Schools as well as a number of other colleges and universities. His most recent publications are *Human Rights and Conflict of Cultures: Freedom of Religion and Conscience in the West and Islam* (with John Kelsay and Abdulaziz Sachedina) and *Ukraine: The Legacy of Intolerance.*

James H. Matlack is director of the Washington office of the American Friends Service Committee (AFSC). He holds a Ph.D. from

Yale University and has taught at Cornell University and the University of Massachusetts. He has held numerous leadership positions in AFSC and traveled extensively for AFSC in Central America, Indochina, and the Middle East.

Yehudah Mirsky is on the staff of the State Department and was formerly director of publications at the Washington Institute for Near East Policy. He holds a J.D. from Yale Law School, where he was an editor of the law review. He writes regularly for the *Economist* on politics and culture, and his essays and reviews have appeared in *Washington Monthly*, *Yale Law Journal*, *Jerusalem Report*, and the *New Leader*.

William Morrisey is the associate editor of *Interpretation: A Journal of Political Philosophy* (Queens College, Flushing, New York). He has written several articles and books, including *Our Culture "Left or Right"* and *Pacifism and the Political Orders* (in preparation).

Michael Nagler is professor emeritus of classics and comparative literature at the University of California at Berkeley (UCB). He founded the Peace and Conflict Studies Program at UCB, where he regularly teaches a course on nonviolence. He has consulted for the United States Institute of Peace and other organizations and at present is collaborating with Eknath Easwaran on a new book on Gandhi.

Charles E. Nelson is vice president of the United States Institute of Peace. Previously, he was an executive in the RAND Corporation's housing and civil justice programs. He has also worked as a senior staff member in the U.S. Agency for International Development and in a private consulting firm as a lawyer, manager, and administrator on economic and social development programs in the Middle East, Africa, and Latin America. He holds an LL.B. from Harvard Law School.

David Novak is the Edgar M. Bronfman Professor of Modern Judaic Studies at the University of Virginia. He holds a Ph.D. from Georgetown University. He served for more than twenty years as a pulpit rabbi and for three years as Jewish chaplain at St. Elizabeths Hospital, National Institute of Mental Health, in Washington, D.C. He has written several books and articles, including *Jewish-Christian Dialogue: A Jewish Justification*.

Abdulaziz Sachedina is a professor of religious studies at the University of Virginia in Charlottesville. He received his Ph.D. from the University of Toronto and from 1974 to 1988 he delivered a series of lectures in East Africa, Pakistan, Europe, and the Middle East on a variety of Muslim and Islamic social, political, and legal themes. His publications include *The Just Ruler in Twelver Shi'ism: The Comprehensive Authority of the Jurist in Imamite Jurisprudence* and *Human Rights and the Conflict of Cultures: Western and Islamic Perspectives on Religious Liberty*.

David Saperstein is the director of the Religious Action Center of Reform Judaism. He is also an attorney and an adjunct professor in comparative Jewish and American law at Georgetown University Law School. His articles on political and social justice issues have appeared in the *Washington Post*, the *New York Times*, and many major general and Jewish periodicals.

David R. Smock is director of the grant program of the United States Institute of Peace. Previously he was executive associate to the president of the United Church of Christ, executive director of International Voluntary Services, and vice president of the Institute of International Education, and he held various positions with the Ford Foundation. He holds a Ph.D. in anthropology from Cornell University and an M.Div. from New York Theological Seminary. He is the author of *Religious Perspectives on War* and editor of *Making War and Waging Peace: Foreign Intervention in Africa*, and author and editor of several books on Africa and the Middle East.

Susan Brooks Thistlethwaite is a professor of theology at the Chicago Theological Seminary. She holds an M.Div. from Duke Divinity School and a Ph.D. from Duke University's Graduate School of Religion. With Mary Potter Engel, she recently edited *Lift Every Voice: Constructing Christian Theologies from the Underside*. Her other books include *A Just Peace Church* and *Sex, Race and God: Christian Feminism in Black and White*.

Joe Volk is the executive secretary for the Friends Committee on National Legislation, Washington, D.C. He currently chairs the Arms Transfer Working Group of the Monday Lobby, an arms control and disarmament lobby group. He is past chair of the Foreign Policy and Military Spending Task Force of the Washington Interreligious Staff Council, an interfaith lobbying group composed of Catholic, Protestant, Jewish, Muslim, and Peace Church representatives. He became persuaded of his pacifist position while resisting the Vietnam War as a private in the U.S. Army.

Walter Wink is professor of biblical interpretation at Auburn Theological Seminary in New York City. In 1989–90 he was a Peace Fellow at the United States Institute of Peace. He is the author of a trilogy, *Naming the Powers*, *Unmasking the Powers*, and *Engaging the Powers*. His other books include *Violence and Nonviolence in South Africa*, *Transforming Bible Study*, *The Bible in Human Transformation*, and *John the Baptist in the Gospel Tradition*.

John Howard Yoder is professor of theology at the University of Notre Dame and a fellow of Notre Dame's Kroc Institute for International Peace Studies. He served the Mennonite denomination in overseas relief and mission administration, in ecumenical representation, and in seminary education. His best-known writings on matters of war and peace are *The Politics of Jesus*, *Nevertheless*, *The Varieties of Religious Pacifism*, *What Would You Do?*, *When War Is Unjust*, *He Came Preaching Peace*, and *The Priestly Kingdom*.

Notes

1. John Mueller, *Retreat from Doomsday: The Obsolescence of Major War* (New York: Basic Books, 1989).

2. The quotations are cited in Evan Luard, *War in International Society* (New Haven: Yale University Press, 1987), p. 368.

3. These features of nonviolent action were in part suggested by Reinhold Niebuhr in *Moral Man and Immoral Society* (New York: Scribner's, 1960), pp. 244–54. Niebuhr should be given special credit for calling attention to the advantages of nonviolence, since he rather powerfully elaborates and acknowledges them in the midst of his famous critique of pacifism.

4. Martin Luther King, Jr., "Nonviolence and Racial Justice," *Christian Century*, February 6, 1957, pp. 165–67.

5. *Transforming Struggle: Strategy and the Global Experience of Nonviolent Direct Action* (Cambridge, MA: Harvard University Center for International Affairs, 1992), pp. 3–6.

6. Walter Wink, *Engaging the Powers: Discernment and Resistance in a World of Domination* (Minneapolis: Fortress Press, 1992), p. 192.

7. John Howard Yoder, *Nevertheless* (Scottdale, PA: Herald Press, 1992).

8. *The Harvest of Justice Is Sown in Peace*, statement by the National Conference of Catholic Bishops, *Origins: CNS Documentary Service*, vol. 23, no. 26 (December 9, 1993), pp. 453–54.

9. David R. Smock, *Religious Perspectives on War: Christian, Muslim, and Jewish Attitudes toward Force after the Gulf War* (Washington, DC: United States Institute of Peace, 1992).

10. Individual papers are available upon request from the United States Institute of Peace.

11. A helpful discussion of the historical background of Christian pacifism can be found in Lisa Sowle Cahill, *Love Your Enemies: Discipleship, Pacifism, and Just War Theory* (Minneapolis: Fortress Press, 1994), pp. 157–75.

12. In John C. Wenger, ed., *The Complete Writings of Menno Simons* (Scottdale, PA: Herald Press, 1955).

13. Cahill, *Love Your Enemies*, p. 166.

14. Cahill, *Love Your Enemies*, p. 169.

15. T. C. Jones, *Fox's Attitude toward War* (Annapolis, MD: Academic Fellowship, 1972), pp. 24–25.

16. Cahill, *Love Your Enemies*, p. 176.

17. Walter Rauschenbusch, *A Theology for the Social Gospel* (Nashville: Abingdon Press, 1945), p. 106.

18. Cahill, *Love Your Enemies*, p. 184.

19. Affiliation for identification purposes only.

20. Abraham Isaac Kook, *Ig'rot Ha-Riyah*, Vol. I (Jerusalem: Mossad Harav Kook, 1962).

21. The Gandhi-Buber exchange may be found in Paul R. Mendes-Flohr, ed., *A Land of Two Peoples: Martin Buber on Jews and Arabs* (New York: Oxford University Press, 1983), pp. 106–26.

United States Institute of Peace

The United States Institute of Peace is an independent, nonpartisan federal institution created and funded by Congress to strengthen the nation's capacity to promote the peaceful resolution of international conflict. Established in 1984, the Institute meets its congressional mandate through an array of programs, including grants, fellowships, conferences and workshops, library services, publications, and other educational activities. The Institute's Board of Directors is appointed by the President of the United States and confirmed by the Senate.

Board of Directors

Chester A. Crocker (Chairman), Distinguished Research Professor of Diplomacy, School of Foreign Service, Georgetown University

Max M. Kampelman, Esq. (Vice Chairman), Fried, Frank, Harris, Shriver and Jacobson, Washington, D.C.

Dennis L. Bark, Senior Fellow, Hoover Institution on War, Revolution and Peace, Stanford University

Thomas E. Harvey, former general counsel, United States Information Agency

Theodore M. Hesburgh, President Emeritus, University of Notre Dame

William R. Kintner, Professor Emeritus of Political Science, University of Pennsylvania

Christopher H. Phillips, former U.S. ambassador to Brunei

Elspeth Davies Rostow, Stiles Professor of American Studies Emerita, Lyndon B. Johnson School of Public Affairs, University of Texas

Mary Louise Smith, civic activist; former chairman, Republican National Committee

W. Scott Thompson, Professor of International Politics, Fletcher School of Law and Diplomacy, Tufts University

Allen Weinstein, President, Center for Democracy, Washington, D.C.

Members ex officio

Ralph Earle II, Deputy Director, U.S. Arms Control and Disarmament Agency

Toby Trister Gati, Assistant Secretary of State for Intelligence and Research

Ervin J. Rokke, Lieutenant General, U.S. Air Force; President, National Defense University

Walter B. Slocombe, Principal Deputy Under Secretary of Defense for Policy

Richard H. Solomon, President, United States Institute of Peace (nonvoting)